Uwe Petersen # The Illusions of Politics

Donald Trump's contribution to overcome them
and the tasks of
European foreign and economic policy

Author: Uwe Petersen

The Illusions of Politics
Donald Trump's contribution to overcome them
and the tasks of
European foreign and economic policy

Translated by Miriam Peters and Rebecca Halbach

Original German Title:

Die Illusionen der Politik
Die Bedeutung Donald Trumps zu deren Überwindung
und die Aufgaben der
europäischen Außen- und Wirtschaftspolitik

Book cover design:
Reinhard Büttner Design & Konzeption

Date of publication: 2018

ISBN: 9781731249166

Kindle

www.philosope.de
Dr. Uwe Petersen
Dubrowstraße 49, 14129 Berlin
Phone: +49308014369, Mail: philosope@arcor.de

Content

A. The illusions of politics, their consequences and Donald Trump's contribution to overcome them

Crucial principles determining our economic and social actions are more and more proving to be illusions, the adherence to which is destroying the economy and society and international relations. They are increasingly perceived as lies. This creates a breeding ground for political charlatans and rat-catchers.

The Trumps, however, cannot only destroy the established economic and social structures. They can, through their actions, also contribute to overcoming the political illusions and uproot entrenched societal structures.

I. The illusion of a lasting community of values between Europe and the US and the reliance on the belief that Europe's security can be ensured by the US through the framework of NATO

During the past 100 years, the world's intellectual, social and economic development was driven by Europe. Europeanism is what I call the synthesis of Christianity and antiquity in all its secular forms. Modern science and technology but also liberalism and Marxism and the capitalist market economy are based on Europeanism.

Ultimately, the role model of Europeanism is the free, self-realizing individual – religiously as the image of God – and his reference back to the world and community. Depending on whether the religious or secular intentions prevail or whether the development of the individual self or of the loving relationship are emphasized, the Europeanism takes different forms. In doing so, the West tends to exaggerate the individual freedom, the East the solidarity and the unity of the people.

The USA developed into the center of Western Europeanism and Russia into the center of Eastern Europeanism. Central Europe has always attempted to combine these two ideals. During the Cold War the Western Europeanism triumphed. Western Europe and, after the collapse of the Eastern bloc, also Eastern Germany and the bordering Eastern European countries felt united with the USA in a community of values which advocated for the self-determination of the people, democracy and the capitalist market economy. This community of values had a military basis in the form of NATO, the North Atlantic Treaty. The leading power of Western Europe and NATO was the US.[1]

---

[1]   Detailed account in Uwe Petersen: *Blessing and Victims of Globalization. Economic and social development, relative empoverishment, unemployment, economic crises, left- and right-wing radicalism, religious wars, refugee streams and Europe's responsibility*, ISBN- 13:978-198377298, p. 37 and following, 90 and following.

Europe's and the USA's community of values is at risk of breaking apart due to the following reasons:

1. the challenging of the values,
2. the different political and economic interests in a changing world.

1. The challenging of the western values by Donald Trump

On the one hand we owe the economic and social progress to Western Europeanism. On the other hand, it is also responsible for:

- the breaking apart of society due to increasingly unequal distribution of property and income and the resulting problems of social impoverishment of the lower social classes,
- the rising risk of a crisis of the world economy,
- Islamism and terrorism as a response to the globalization of Europeanism,
- environmental pollution and climate issues and
- the streams of refugees.

However, because the political and economic establishment justifies the current situation with Western European values and proclaims it as having no alternative due to the given economic conditions and power relations, it is perceived as a lie by the lower classes.

As a result, radicals promising *alternative* policies inspire an audience in almost all countries. With Donald Trump, a president was elected in the US who challenged established values relating to economic trade, international treaties and mannerisms and thereby removes the US as a guarantor for the western societal and economic order.

2. Different political and economic interests in a changing world

Despite the "community of values" differences between Europe and the US as to economic and political interests have also persisted and the US has never shied away from using its geopolitical dominance on an economic level. It was, however restrained from the unscrupulous abuse of its position of power through the common values and principles. Moreover, the US feels responsible for the world and aspired to also introduce less developed countries and such countries which were not governed democratically and committed to human rights, to the western way of life.

However, the more the US itself is suffering under trade deficits, deindustrialization, relative impoverishment of the less qualified and the influx of economic migrants, the stronger the desire becomes to

- interfere administratively in foreign trade relations, to pursue autocracy or manage economic relations through bilateral deals
- withdraw oneself from the world in terms of foreign policy, to limit oneself

to the USA and to engage in a purely nationalist one in the spirit of Trump's slogan "America first",

- also employ economic power in the form of sanctions, and in fact also by blackmail of other states or undertakings to comply with US interests and sanctions because otherwise they are not permitted to operate on the American market.

Due to this desire, Donald Trump increasingly tends to interfere with international trade if he considers the US to be disadvantaged, to withdraw the US from all international conflicts and to leave the conflicts to those affected. In any case, Trump uses the economic power of the US and wants to enforce his will internationally through the threat and imposition of sanctions. Only when the conflicts could also undermine the security of the US, does Trump threaten radical military intervention.

Given that, as a real estate broker, he thinks in deals and profit and loss, he likes to make decisions based on what the US has so far spent or will spend on certain countries and the extent to which it receives something in return. Thus, he asks, to some extent rightly, what America contributes to the NATO budget and to what extent other countries bear those costs and has already floated the possibility to withdraw from NATO and other international agreements. Furthermore, Donald Trump is erratic and quite resistant to advice and makes tweeting and lying his identifying feature. Like this he shakes the whole present world order.

He can, however, also dissolve deadlocked situations and power relations and make economic and social development possible. For the other states, on the other hand, he becomes unpredictable and forces them to react accordingly and to progressively denounce the community of values with the US.

II. The illusion that the introduction of a parliamentary democracy guarantees a harmonious development of a people anywhere and the possible contribution of Donald Trump to overcoming it

The conversion of the rest of the world to a western individualistic attitude to life, to a parliamentary democratic form of government, to a legal system guided by humanism and a free capitalist market economy, was a significant driving force for western globalization.

The history of the so-called *Arab Spring* shows very clearly the conditionality of the conviction that a parliamentary democracy guarantees a peaceful and evolving society. The development in Tunisia where the *Arab* Spring started is the only example which could be considered as a confirmation of this theory to some extent. In all other countries the attempt has failed painfully.

In Libya old tribal allegiances reignited in combination with Islamist tendencies. In Egypt radical Islamists used the free elections to establish an Islamist regime and in Syria Islamists were equally threatening to take power.

In Egypt this development could virtually only be prevented through a military coup with the consequence that Egypt is an even more radical military dictatorship today than it was in Mubarak's time or at least a democracy driven by the military with a radical suppression of all Islamist tendencies.

In Syria and Iraq relatively, secular social structures could only establish in the areas controlled by Kurds and their allies, areas which are, however, to be reclaimed by the Assad Regime with the aid of Iran and Russia. Other than that, a relatively secular governance form is that of Bashar al Assad himself. However, it is only socially supported by the Alawites, Christian and other non-Sunni sects, although to some extent also by the Sunni intelligence and Sunni enterprises. The majority of the Sunnis rejects the Assad regime. Though insofar as the areas "liberated" by insurgency movements from Assad's military dictatorship are not recaptured by the Assad regime with Russian and Iranian help, they are mostly governed by Islamists.

In western countries it was long believed or was made to be believed by the media that the insurgents were guided by western principles until it became clearer and clearer that the driving forces among them were Islamists who differed only slightly from IS fighters.

The vast losses of human life and destruction in the recapture of the Aleppo and other areas through Assad were lamented. Much less attention was paid to the fact that the fanatic resistance, which did not even shy away from human shields, primarily by the Islamists, was also responsible for it.

But who in the world, apart from the Islamists themselves, would profit from it if these Islamists had seized power?

The western countries must learn that the societal systems have to be made by or at least supported by the people themselves. One example that even an erratic president cannot do everything if democratic views are ingrained in the institutions of the people, is the US itself. However, if they are not so ingrained, then archaic social systems or military or party dictatorships develop, although the latter are the smaller evil because they at least create peace and order and therefore the prerequisites for possible economic prosperity. The remarkable example for this is the People's Republic of China.

As unbearable as the reign of Assad in Syria is for the democrats who are influenced by western values, it must, despite all his crimes, not be forgotten that his opponents have acted the same way within their area of control and, had they won power completely in Syria, they would have advanced with the same brutality against the groups which used to support Assad.

What is said for Syria applies to all countries by analogy. Freedom fighters against suppression and corruption, like Mugabe in Zimbabwe or Enrique Santos in Nicaragua, rapidly turned into corrupt suppressors after having obtained power.

Those who were suppressed before tend to suppress even stricter when they are more driven by principles than the established regimes, also because they have to shatter the established structures. Considering the rule of the Jacobins after the *French Revolution* and the course of action of the Bolsheviks after the *Russian October Revolution*.

The attempts of the West, and in particular of the US, to help non-European countries to establish a western democratic system and attitude to life have already failed in Afghanistan, Iraq and Libya and presumably would have also done so in Syria. It must be conceded, subject to all reservations, to Vladimir Putin that he has stabilized the Russian Federation and the relations with most of the former member states of the Soviet Union and prevented social chaos and economic need, although partly with questionable methods.

The Russian Empire may just not be governed in any other way. That is already evident by the fact that the other successor states to the USSR are also governed through an autocracy and this is also the case in the socialist Eastern Asian countries. Undoubtedly military rule is also necessary for Syria. This is why Putin is probably right that under these circumstances, if need be through the Assad regime, Syria needs to be pacified.

A democracy can only work if the voters let themselves be guided by rational considerations and the common good and in doing so consider legitimate interests of minorities. If they only act on emotions, egoism or tribal allegiance, then a dictatorship may be necessary, simply to create peace in a region. A democracy which does not comply with the given criteria, quickly creates chaotic conditions and a call for a "strong leader" anyway.

Applied to the "Arab Spring", it was a mistake on the side of the West to contribute to the destabilization of the regime in Libya and Syria. In Iraq too, after the elimination of Saddam Hussein, the Baath party ruling until then should not have been destroyed but integrated in the new order. The most disastrous one was the US approach in Afghanistan when it supported Islamism against the Soviet Union and thereby lead Afghanistan into chaos more than ever.

In Syria the western support to rebel groups which were ultimately ruled by Islamists significantly increased the destruction and the number of deaths. Every obstruction to the retaking of rebel territory held by Islamist groups, whether they are called IS, Al Qaeda, Al Nusra front or whatever else, prolongs the suffering of the Syrian people and sets refugees on the move.

The only exception was the support to the Kurds who established a relatively secular system, however provoking the Turks by doing so. Nevertheless, there will not be peace if the Turks and the Kurds do not agree on a modus vivendi.

1. The unresolved Korea question and the possible contribution of Donald Trump to resolve it.

Since the Korean War nearly 70 years ago there is no peace treaty between North and South Korea and the relationship of North Korea with the US and most other countries in the world is unresolved. The ceasefire with North Korea which leads smaller conflicts time and time again, was also signed by the US in the name of 15 countries participating in the war on the side of the Americans. Thereby the US has a central importance for the easing of the international relations with North Korea.

With the reference to Bloomberg it is reported that there are only 24 foreign embassies in Pyongyang (among them also Germany and the United Kingdom) while the Swedish mission is the unofficial seat of the US, Canada and Australia. >> the other embassies mainly take on humanitarian tasks. Conversely North Korea maintains an embassy in 47 countries, for example in Spain, Italy and many African countries <<[2]

Due to the principles that an American president does not meet with a "rogue state" or rather, as it were, that the terrain for a meeting between the heads of state must first be established by subordinates, North Korea's aspiration of nuclear power and its development of intercontinental missiles turned into, in Barack Obama's words, the "problem which was the most difficult to solve" for America and the neighboring countries. The US and the surrounding states consider the armament of North Korea a threat to international peace. The Kim dynasty and its followers probably only want to protect themselves from a violent overthrow with support from abroad. Iraq and Libya are warning examples for this.

What does Donald Trump do? He starts a smear campaign, threatens North Korea with obliteration and strengthens economic sanctions. At the same time, he blackmails entrepreneurs from other countries who also do business in the US into joining this boycott and encourages North Korea's neighboring countries, China and Russia to also exercise economic pressure on North Korea. Then he meets with North Korea's President Kim Jong-un and agrees with him that the Korean peninsula will become free of nuclear weapons, a peace treaty will be concluded and that the sanctions are to be lifted. As a preliminary gesture he stops joint military maneuvers with South Korea and neighboring states. As a result, the relationship with North Korea is more relaxed and North Korea virtually recognized as a fully-fledged state.

Although Donald Trump, as usual, celebrates this "deal" as a great success and proclaims North Korea's nuclear disarmament, the military position of North Korea will unlikely change. North Korea will not surrender the military power it gained and will also be able to uphold this position because the agreement also contains that

---

[2]   https://www.businessinsider.de/diese-staaten-arbeiten-mit-nordkorea-zusammen-und-koennten-fuer-trump-zum-problem-werden-2017-5

the US must withdraw their military troops from South Korea and dismantle the nuclear weapons there which will already not happen because the mutual mistrust is still great.

Nevertheless, one can talk of an easing of the relationship with North Korea. Even if the US maintain the sanctions, Russia and China and more and more states will take this easing as an occasion to intensify economic relations with North Korea bit by bit. Through its attained military strength North Korea will use the acquired technological competence to develop the private sector and thus slowly rise to a fully-fledged industrial power and after accession to the Non-Proliferation Treaty, which prohibits the passing-on of know-how on nuclear weapons, to a recognized nuclear power. The better North Korea does economically, the more saturated it becomes so that the wish to maintain prosperity will progressively discourage North Korea from international adventures.

However, the more the US withdraws from the Pacific region, the more the Pacific states' who until now believed themselves to be under the nuclear shield of the US, desire grows to strengthen their own defense efforts and to also become a nuclear power. The latter is at least to be presumed of Japan.

South Korea will balance its position between North Korea, Japan and China. Thus, overall a multi-polar situation is created in Eastern Asia. On the one hand China, at first, experiences an increase in power within the region but, if China should abuse its power, it could potentially lead to counter-alliances to compensate. In the same way as communist Vietnam is today not necessarily seen as a friend of China but rather relies on the USA, its former enemy, the saturated North Korea could equally be more open for closer relations with the US and Japan. Donald Trump could thus, through his meeting with the North Korean ruler Kim Jong-un, have given the Eastern Asian region the stimulus for creating peace.

2. The Near and Middle East conflict and the possible contribution of Donald Trump to its solution

The Near and Middle East is a bundle of diverse interests and sub-conflicts which is nearly impossible to disentangle. Fundamental differences of faith within Islam, in particular between the Sunni and Shiites which are, unlike in Christianity, *not from this world* but strive for a theocracy, are overshadowed by the nationalistic Turkish dreams of the revival of the Ottoman Empire and by a resistance against western secularization and against Israel's Zionism.

Since the partition of Palestine, the Palestine conflict has been brewing. Thousands of Palestinians have left the territory of Israel and live in refugee camps in Lebanon, Jordan and in the Gaza Strip. Due to natural population growth the number of refugees has since increased from 700,000 to 5,000,000 who dream of being able to migrate to Israel again, a completely illusionary expectation but a brewing potential for conflict.

Israel progressively expand into the Palestinian territory with its settlements. The Palestinians cultivate their trauma of persecution or rather terrorize themselves in the Gaza Strip, supported by Iran. The world objects and appeals to the parties in the conflict to agree on the two State solution. Without success.

Since that time the refugees and their descendants are being economically supported with billions and billions worldwide. Thus, those unhealthy circumstances become chronic. If the refugees had not been supported, the misery may have become so great that a bearable solution could have been coerced and in particular more advantageous ones for the Palestinians than is possible today given that Israel's building of settlements is being expanded continuously. How long is this supposed to go on?

What does Donald Trump do? He recognizes the deadlocked situation and increases the pressure on the parties to find a solution by moving the US embassy from Tel Aviv to Jerusalem and cutting financial aid for the Palestinians. If all other countries were to follow the US and at the same time put pressure on Israel, for example that the US would threaten to also freeze financial support to Israel, then negotiations for the resolution of the conflict could possibly be forced.

As Colonel Gaddafi in Libya and Saddam Hussein in Iraq have been overthrown, the internal tensions in those countries became even more poisoned and plunged the countries into chaos. The *Arab Spring* of which the western World had hoped that it would bring democratization and the Islamists that it would bring an Islamization of the secular military dictatorships in the Near East, resulted in the restauration of a military dictatorship in Egypt and lead to political, economic and military chaos in Libya and Syria.

In Syria and in Iraq the US confined itself to supporting relatively secular Kurds and the fight against the IS. At the same time Trump tends to take over the position of Russia that the Assad regime, as cruel as it proceeded against its enemies, is the lesser evil as compared to the Islamist groups and therefore that the internationally recognized Syria should be restored.

A particular danger to peace in the Near East is considered to be the development of Iran. Through negotiations going on for many years it was possible to prevent Iran from developing a nuclear bomb. Nevertheless, it must be assumed that Iran has not abandoned this intention and will resume at the very latest after the termination of the agreement in 2024.

A significant part of a modern military power is the possession of powerful missiles, but not only militarily but also in relation to space projects. Through the vigorous enhancement of its missiles Iran will of course also be feared as threatening peace in future. Furthermore, Iran is expanding its military influence to Syria, the

Hezbollah in Lebanon even into Yemen by which especially Israel and Saudi Arabia feel threatened.

What does Trump do? He pulls the US out of the nuclear deal with Iran, reinstates the previous sanctions and even intensifies them. At the same time, he uses the economically huge American market as a weapon by coercing other countries and undertakings to sever economic contact with Iran on their part and thus to steer Iran into a situation of great economic hardship. This hardship is aimed at increasing the discontent of the people and encourage them to rise up against their government and their system.

After having taken a big enough risk with the threatened and implemented sanctions he offers the President of Iran negotiations without any preconditions and hopes to solve the Iran problem with a "deal".

A further source of danger is Turkey:

- the unresolved question about the Kurds,
- the dreams of a revival of the Ottoman Empire spurred on by President Erdogan and
- President Erdogan's dictatorial measures against the opposition and perceived enemies of Turkey the victims of which are also foreign nationals

Through his policies Erdogan has made foreign states his opponents in multiple ways and is also economically weakened due to Turkey's high debt burden towards foreign countries incurred for the financing of the economic growth.

As Donald Trump was annoyed with Erdogan because he detained an American preacher and did not abide by an exchange agreement, he implements a wide range of economic sanctions against Turkey which weaken Turkey even more and puts it in a precarious economic position.

The heavy application of economic sanctions as a means of foreign policy without consent of the UN Security Council may create a new external situation and uncertainty of external relations. Nevertheless, Donald Trump could achieve through his measures that the economic hardship in Iran and in Turkey becomes so great and that Russia will also suffer hard under it that the Middle East conflict can be resolved more easily. That way the unconventional way Donald Trump is doing politics could still further world peace.

On the other hand, this policy forces the remainder of the states to become progressively more independent from the US by making themselves self-sufficient to a large extent and to rely on each other more. Europe, Russia, China and India could work together more. The remaining countries which can also no longer rely on the US would re-orientate themselves towards this new economic bloc. The Chinese project to revive the Silk road could be given an additional boost.

The precondition for this would be that Europe sets aside its reservations regarding Russia and pushes for a compromise on the Ukraine question. Thus, the US's power to coerce the rest of the world would disappear in the long term.

The closer cooperation between the Eurasian countries and the disappearance of the possibility to coerce could – in the end again thanks to Trump – further world peace.

III. The illusion that Russia could return Crimea to Ukraine and that the sanctions against Russia can be maintained, and the possible contribution of Donald Trump to overcome it

Everyone who assesses the circumstances realistically knows that Crimea which, depending on the interpretation has acceded to Russia or was annexed by Russia, will not be returned to Ukraine. Despite this the Russia policies of western countries proceeds with the illusion that Russia can be forced to do so through sanctions. The statements of western countries on the topic suggest that Russia is an aggressive state which wants to expand west and reincorporate the former Soviet Republics into its domain and thus that the Baltic states but also Poland are under threat next.

In order to better understand Russian politics Russia's actual motives should be made clear from European history through which it becomes even more clear at the same time that Russia can never give back Crimea due to its own self-image.

Russia and Ukraine have a common origin, the Kiev Rus. As Wikipedia writes >> The Kiev Rus (...[3]) was a great medieval empire which is considered as the predecessor state of today's Russia, Ukraine and Belarus. The expression can also be understood as the term for the period in the history of the Rus in which the Kiev, as the seat of the grand duke, was the political and cultural center of the Rurikids dynasty. <<[4]

>> Modern Russian and Belarus scholarship tends to use the collective term old-Russian state (Древнерусское государство). The reason for that is that the term "Kievan Rus" traditionally comprises the begin of statehood in Novgorod under Rurik before the relocation of the capital to Kiev in 882 but does not consider it in its name.<<[5]

>>Through the trade which was principally directed through Constantinople, despite initial conquest attempts on the part of the Rus, close contacts with Byzantium developed which lead to Christian missionary work and eventually in the year 988 during the reign of Vladimir the Holy to the conversion of the Rus to Orthodox faith.<<[6]

---

[3] Erich Donnert: *Das Kiewer Russland: Kultur und Geistesleben vom 9. bis zum beginnenden 13. Jahrhundert.* (Kievan Russia: culture and intellectual life from the 9th to the beginning of the 13th century.) Urania-Verlag, 1983

[4] https://de.wikipedia.org/wiki/Kiewer_Rus

[5] Ibid.

[6] Ibid.

>>Due to the political fragmentation the Old-Russian Empire in the years 1237 to 1240, succumbed to the invasion of the Mongols who made the Rus subject to paying tribute to their Empire of the Golden Horde. The north-eastern part of the Rus (dukedom of Vladimir-Susdal, Rjasan, Twer) remained under their rule until 1480 while the south-western territories and the Galicia-Wolhynien, as a result of the battle on the Irpin River (1321) and the battle on the Blue Waters (1362) came under the rule of the grand duchy of Lithuania which later formed a common Republic with Poland, the Polish-Lithuanian Republic. Areas of today's Ukraine thus came within the polish domain from the 16th century. In the East, the duchy Vladimir-Susdal turned into the grand duchy Moscow which consolidated all Russian neighboring duchies around it step by step and finally conquered the tartar Khanat Kasan. Through that expansion, Ukraine became the rival territory and border territory between Russia and Poland. In the area of the Black Sea the rule of the Crimean khanate was still long upheld under Ottoman sovereignty until Crimea was annexed by the Russian Empire in the 18th century.<<[7]

>>Legal discrimination, economic exploitation and religious pressure on the orthodox population of the south-western Rus by the Polish Crown and the Polish tycoons again and again led to bloody uprisings and against Polish rule which were further spurred on in 1596 by the imposed Church Union of Brest. In the year 1648 the Ukrainiand liberated themselves with a popular uprising under the leadership of the Cossack Hetman Bohdan Chmelnyzkyj from Polish rule and the Zaporozhian Cossacks founded an independent state, the Hetmanate. In 1654 the Cossacks, through the treaty of Pereiaslav submitted themselves to the authority of the Tsar of Moscow and as a result The Ukrainian territory on the left bank (in relation to the Dnieper river), together with Kiev, came under Russian rule.<<[8]

Only >> after the Russian February Revolution in 1917 [note: so nearly 300 years later] and during the German and Austrian occupation at the end of the First World War short-lived Ukrainian nation states, the Ukrainian People's Republic and West-Ukrainian People's Republic emerged. On 22 January 1919 the unification of the two people's republics was approved. The territory of the West-Ukrainian People's Republic was however also claimed by Poland and occupied fully until July 1919 during the Polish-Ukrainian war; however, the Polish troops were pushed back shortly after during the Polish-Soviet war. As a result, the western Ukrainian territories fell to Poland, Romania and Czechoslovakia, central, eastern and southern Ukraine to the Russian Soviet Republic....

During the course of the very eventful and bloody Russian civil war most Ukrainian territories were conquered by the Red Army and, under Trotsky, annexed to Soviet Russia. With the founding of the Soviet Union in December 1922 the Ukrainian SSR was established. <<[9]

---

[7]   https://de.wikipedia.org/wiki/Ukraine
[8]   Ibid.
[9]   Ibid.

>> After the war the whole Ukraine for united under one state, the Soviet Union, for the first time. In the year 1954, on the occasion of the 300-year anniversary of the Pereiaslav agreement the Crimean peninsula was transferred from the Russian to the Ukrainian Soviet Republic.<<[10]

>> The 300th anniversary was celebrated in the USSR with festivities lasting months in the context of which the Ukrainian SSR received the peninsula of Crimea as a present from Khrushchev – present that causes tensions until today. The "unbreakable friendship" of the two "sister people" which were interconnected "forever" by Pereiaslav, the progressiveness of events and the supposed desire, not only of Chmelnyzkyjs but also of the entire Ukrainian people, for re-unification with Russia were emphasized.<<[11]

>>Nikita Khrushchev came from a western Russian farming family which migrated to the Donets Basin in Ukraine in 1908, at the time the most important coal and industrial area in the Russian Empire<<[12], and began his political career in Ukraine.

>>With the dissolution of the Soviet Union Ukraine, following a referendum with an approval rate of 90.3%, gained its official independence in December 1991. Since then it searches for its national identity and its international role between a western orientation, for example an integration in the European Union, and an eastern orientation i.e. a political orientation towards Russia.<<[13]

The collapse of the Soviet Union at first paralyzed the eastern European self- and societal image. Salvation was expected from the West and thus the West tried to spread its view of the world and society to the eastern European countries and Russia. At first the consequence was an even greater collapse of the economy and a disintegration of the Soviet Union into different countries with more or less autocratic regimes, led by former party secretaries of the Communist Party of the Soviet Union. Russia itself was also at risk of falling apart into several independent autonomous republics, some with Islamist tendencies.

Of course, Vladimir Putin is not a "flawless democrat". But could such a person have prevented that the Russian Federation ends in chaos and economic deprivation? Putin succeeded in halting the process of disintegration and reversing and in making Russia a confident factor in international politics again today. But the more he succeeded in doing this the more, the less Russia was considered a playground for the realization of a western social and economic order, in fact not even perceived as an equal partner but a again a threat.

Even though Russia could expect that after the reunification of Germany and the end of the Cold War the eastern European countries would not be accepted into the

---

[10]   https://de.wikipedia.org/wiki/Ukraine
[11]   https://de.wikipedia.org/wiki/Vertrag_von_Perejaslaw
[12]   https://de.wikipedia.org/wiki/Nikita_Sergejewitsch_Chruschtschow
[13]   https://de.wikipedia.org/wiki/Ukraine

western European Union and NATO and that NATO would not advance up to the borders of Russia, exactly that occurred.

A significant part in the termination of the Cold War was the Treaty on Conventional Armed Forces in Europe which was signed on 19 November 1990 by the countries: Belgium, Bulgaria, Denmark, Germany, France, Greece, Iceland, Italy, Canada, Luxembourg, Netherlands, Norway, Poland, Portugal, Romania, Spain, Czechoslovakia, Turkey, the Hungarians, Soviet Union, Great Britain and the USA.>> During a summit of the Organization for Security and Co-operation in Europe (OSCE) in Istanbul the parties to the CFE finally concluded on 19 November 1999 an agreement to adjust the CFE treaty. (A-CFE)<<[14]

Vladimir Putin expressed the disappointment of a lacking realization of this treaty in the following words at the security conference in Munich in 2007: >>The modified treaty on Conventional Armed Forces in Europe was signed in 1999. It takes into account the new geopolitical reality – the liquidation of the Warsaw Pact. Since then seven years have passed and only four states have ratified this document, among them the Russian Federation.

The NATO countries have openly proclaimed that they will not ratify the treaty, including the determination of limits on armed forces of a certain strength being stationed on the borders, until Russia closes down its military bases in Moldova and Georgia. Our troops withdraw from Georgia, even with accelerated speed. We have resolved those problems with our Georgian colleagues as should be known to everyone. In Moldova one unit of one and a half thousand drafted men who undertake tasks to promote peace and guard ammunition depots which are left from the time of the USSR remain. We are constantly in talks with Mr. Solana on these issues and he knows are position. We are prepared to continue working in this direction.

But what is happening at the same time? In Bulgaria and Romania so-called minor American outposts with 5000 men each are formed. That means that NATO brings its forced closer and closer to our borders and we, who strictly comply with the treaty, do not react in any way to this action.

I think it is apparent that the process of the NATO enlargement bears no relation to the modernization of the alliance itself or to safeguarding security in Europe. On the contrary, it is a provoking factor which lowers the level of mutual trust. Now we have the right to ask: Against whom is this enlargement? And what has become of those assurances the western partners gave us after the dissolution of the Warsaw Treaty. Where are these declarations now? We do not even remember them anymore. But I permit myself, before this audience, to recall what has been said. I would like to cite a quote from an appearance of the NATO Secretary General, Mr. Wörner, on 17 May 1990 in Brussels. Back then he said: "Alone the fact that we are ready not to station the NATO forces behind the borders of the Federal Republic of Germany gives the Soviet Union firm safety guarantees." Where are these guarantees?

---

[14] https://sicherheitspolitik.bpb.de/m7/articles/m7-06

The rocks and the concrete blocks of the Berlin Wall have long become souvenirs. But one must not forget that its fall was also made possible thanks to the historic choice, also of our people, the people of Russia, a choice for the benefit of democracy and freedom, of openness and real partnership with all members of the large European family.

Now it is attempted to again impose new lines of division and walls upon us – albeit virtual ones, but equally divisive ones which divide our whole continent. Is it going to have to again take many years and decades and the change of several generations of politicians to "dismantle" those new walls? <<[15]

At first Russia still believed to be respected, as part of the easing of tensions, as an equal member of western European organizations. This hope was dispersed at the latest when the eastern European antiballistic defense systems were to be set up. The West may claim that these are intended to intercept missiles from the Middle and Far East. However, Russia was not involved in these systems and the Russian proposal to simply install the stations on Russian territory was denied.

At the security conference in 2007 in Munich Vladimir Putin said on this point: >> We are also concerned about plans to set up parts of a missile defense system in Europe. Who needs a new round to an, in this case inevitable, arms race? I deeply doubt that it is the Europeans themselves.

None of these so-called "problem countries" has missiles which, in order to threaten Europe, would have to have a range of 5000-8000 kilometers. And in the foreseeable future they will not have any, not even the prospect of them. Even the hypothetical launch of a North Korean missile in the direction of the territory of the USA across western Europe defies all laws of ballistics. As we say in Russia, this is like "scratching one's right ear with the left hand". <<[16]

It is obvious that due to these experiences Russia in turn had to also consider its own security and reacted increasingly sensitively to acts of any kind by means of which the European Union and NATO nudged towards its borders and incorporated former Soviet republics into their systems. Russia knew that no country could be admitted to NATO which had internal conflicts and therefore supported, also militarily, Abkhazia and South Ossetia in their fight for independence from Georgia, when Georgia wanted to forcefully take over these countries in 1992. Russia, however, did not accept these countries wishes to become constituent republics of the Russian Federation. Thus, they were de facto independent but according to Georgian claims part of Georgia and this simmering conflict made it impossible for Georgia to be admitted to NATO.

Due to the common history set out Russia had to react particularly sensitively to ambitions which would have led Ukraine into the European Union and NATO.

---

[15]   http://www.ag-friedensforschung.de/themen/Sicherheitskonferenz/2007-putin-dt.html
[16]   Ibid.

Ukraine may have had a common origin with Russia but at the same time many influences from Poland and Lithuania. Thus, the Ukrainian society is divided. The western part is mostly catholic or Ukrainian-Orthodox or rather autonomous orthodox, speaks Ukrainian and leans more towards the West, the eastern part mostly Russian-Orthodox and leans more towards Russia.

>>Russian mother tongue speakers make up the linguistic majority in the autonomous Republic of Crimea and in Sevastopol with 77.0% and 90.6% respectively. Many Russian native speakers in the Crimea are ethnic Ukrainians and relatives of other minorities. In Oblast Donezk and Oblast Luhansk the proportion of Russian native speakers is 74.9% and 68.8% respectively.<<[17]

---

[17] https://de.wikipedia.org/wiki/Ukraine

Region	Orthodox				Catholic			Protest.
		Patriarch Moskow	Patriarch Kiev	autonomous[20]		Greek cath.	Roman cath.	
Western	%	%	%	%	%	%	%	%
Lviv	31,3	2,1	16,0	13,2	57,6	53,0	4,6	6,8
Ivano-Frankivsk	35,7	2,3	22,4	11,1	53,4	50,9	2,4	5,2
Ternopil	37,9	7,2	14,0	16,8	51,1	46,2	4,9	8,1
Eastern								
Donezk	47,3	40,9	4,9	0,3	2,8	1,9	0,9	29,8
Charkiv	49,3	44,2	2,5	1,6	1,7	0,9	0,9	29,2
Luhansk	56,1	50,7	3,6	0,8	0,5	0,4	0,1	25,3
Crimea	42,4	38,0	2,9	0,7	1,7	0,7	1,0	16,9
City Swastopol	49,1	44,8	1,7	0,9	3,4	2,6	0,9	25,9
Ukraine	54,6	36,9	13,3	3,8	14,4	11,5	2,9	19,8

Moreover, under Viktor Juschtschenko >>an active policy of Ukranization was conducted; for example, Russian was driven back in schools and in daily life and many measures were introduced which were intended to promote the use of the Ukrainian language. The President Janukowytsch elected in 2010, however lifted

---

18 Report on registered religious communities, performed by "Institute for Religious Freedom" (IRF), a nongovernmental organization; status: 1 January 2010

19 Source: https://de.wikipedia.org/wiki/Religionen_in_der_Ukraine

20 >> After the proclamation of the first independent Ukrainian state on 25 January 1918, the Ukrainian People's Republic, the Ukrainian clergy attempted to reinforce the governmental independence with the establishment of an autonomous orthodox church. ... in 1937 it no longer existed. After the German occupation during the Second World War an autonomous Ukrainian church was founded for a second time in the German administered part of Poland (Generalgouvernement). ... Before the advance of the Red Army the church hierarchy fled to the west in 1944 without exception, it remained prohibited in the Ukrainian SSR. ... The starting point this time was the Polish-Orthodox church who had been awarded the autonomous status by the Patriarch of Constantinople in 1924. It was reorganized first among emigrants, first in Germany, then in the US and Canada. In 1949 there were 80 communities in Germany. In the 1950s many Ukrainians emigrated to the US, Canada, Australia, South America and other countries in Western Europe. In these countries Ukrainian-Orthodox church communities were established. ...In 1990 the Ukrainian autonomous Orthodox church was officially established again in Ukraine again and fused with the foreign eparchies. The Patriarch Mstyslav (Skrypnyk) from the USA became the head. ... In 1995 the churches in the USA, western Europe and Australia split from the Ukrainian church and formed separate churches. ... Since 2015 the church no longer has a leading metropolitan. << https://de.wikipedia.org/wiki/Ukrainische_Autokephale_Orthodoxe_Kirche

many of these measures again against which the opposition around Julija Tymo-schenko protested vehemently.<<[21]

When Vladimir Putin's offers of concessions from beneficial energy prices to large loans to Ukraine did not bear fruit and Ukraine turned, basically through a coup against the sitting president Janukowytsch, as a result of the Maidan protests towards the West, Putin could only prevent this development by supporting, as before in Georgia, the discontent of the Russian-leaning population against Ukranization measures. This is how the bloody conflicts in the eastern part of Ukraine came about.

Despite being mostly Russian speaking and Russian-Orthodox, Crimea was pre-sented to Ukraine by Khrushchev on the occasion of the 300-year anniversary of the agreement of Pereiaslav so to speak as security of the indestructible community be-tween Russia and Ukraine. Through Ukraine turning its back on Russia the basis for this gift fell away. At the same time Russia had to fear that it may also have had to withdraw its Black Sea fleet from Sevastopol. This is what led to the incorporation of Crimea by Russia.

From the argumentation so far, it should have become clear that Russia does not want to annex Ukraine, in fact not even the rebellious Donetz region. On the contrary Russia was to prevent that Ukraine is incorporated into the western alliances and Ukraine turns into the deployment zone of NATO. A solution could therefore only be to neutralize Ukraine, a position which would open economically interesting pro-spects as a bridge between East and West. Crimea is, however, lost for Ukraine.

As long as this is not recognized and the Western countries continue to try to also force the return of Crimea through sanctions the European countries obstruct their own policy, the economic exchange with Russia and the Ukrainian population must continue to suffer.

Although the US are among the greatest enemies of Russia, the impediments to free trade relations and the increasing alienation between Europe and the US caused by Donald Trump, force the Europeans to intensify relations with Russia. Donald Trump is however emotionally and possibly also commercially tied to Russia. Thus, he could also, contrary to the prevailing American Russia-phobia, order a loosening of sanctions and thereby force the western countries even more to normalize relations with Russia.

---

[21] https://de.wikipedia.org/wiki/Ukraine

IV. The illusion that a generous intake of refugees is possible and the contribution of extreme right-wing and left-wing Trumpists to overcome this illusion

In principle anyone who caringly approaches other people and therefore also refugees is to be praised, and anyone who fosters ethnic arrogance and is xenophobic is to be reprimanded. However, principles are static and can only determine actions *in principle* and, as shown, also lead to illusions.

Because with refugees who stream into other countries diverse problems can occur, inter alia when

1. the hosting people do not *want* to be caring. In principle it can be assumed that the majority of people is open to the need of others. This openness, however, can also turn into rejection, even hate if

2. the foreigners insist on their own mannerisms with which they cause irritation on the part of the locals such as

    a. concealment of the face,

    b. discrimination of women, objection to female teachers, doctors and supervisors,

    c. different conceptions of cleanliness and other forms of living together,

    d. aggressiveness or even potential terrorism

3. refugees are better supported by the government than locals in need,

4. the number of refugees becomes so high that it is perceived as foreign infiltration of the familiar home,

5. the state is not willing or is incapable of registering and integrating the refugees properly, to guarantee the safety of the people and abandons small communities with the problems caused there as it was unfortunately also the case in Germany.

The tolerance level is relatively high in the larger industrial towns and relatively low in smaller communities with fairly uniform, traditional ways of life. If the tolerance level is exceeded, the result is opposition by the local population which can in turn lead to additional aggressiveness of refugees.

In Europe and even in the relatively open societies of northern Europe the tolerance level is apparently crossed more and more. The consequence is that the trust in the established powers diminishes and populist radical right and left-wing parties grow.

In this case Trumps can also be necessary in order to get the problems under control. Thus, the Hungarian Prime Minister, Viktor Orbán, was first reprimanded when he reinforced the Hungarian border with barbed wire. Italian politicians are accused of preventing rescue operations in the Mediterranean even though everyone knows that if the different horrible dangers on the way through Africa and across the Mediterranean did not exist and not as many accidents occurred, the stream of refugees and the destabilization of the European countries would be even greater.

The strengthening of radical right- and left-wing parties is like a disease a wake-up call that the current way of dealing with refugees is not appropriate and leads to the destruction of one's own society and thus ultimately does not help the refugees either.

V. The illusion that general prosperity is promoted through further liberalization of world trade, its consequences and the contribution of Donald Trump to overcome it

It is a fundamental belief of market economics scholarship that international trade increases the peoples' standard of living. If every country specializes in the production of the goods which it can, in comparison to other countries, produce cheaper then all countries profit.

The advantage of international trade applies only if the production conditions of the relevant countries is natural, so for example amber from the Baltic Sea is exchanged for bananas in South America. Because amber is probably not found much in South America and bananas could only be grown in the Baltic Sea countries at great costs in greenhouses. Equally both trade partners will profit if, for example Iceland, produces aluminum with cheap thermal energy and trades it for wine from Italy.

This production advantage on the side of Great Britain and actually all industrial countries increases more and more relative to the trade partners with slower technical progress during the course of the economic development because the profits drawn from it can advance industrialization and the technical know-how can be the basis for further innovations. Even agriculture benefits from technical advances. Today many agricultural products can be produced more cheaply in industrial countries than in developing countries and the sale to those countries can destroy the local industry there.

In order to operate the technologically more advanced systems the level of education in industrial countries rises simultaneously. More and more diverse qualifications develop. The more secular knowledge required for the development of the means of production, furthermore, leads to a greater individualization of people, a precondition for a democratic system.

In the less developed countries, on the other hand, the people remain at a low level of education and in archaic tribal and familial relationships. Insofar as workers with higher qualifications are trained in developing countries, they still do not find enough jobs today and try to migrate to the industrialized countries. This way a relatively left-behind civilization can be maintained. At the same time, however, the potential migration to industrial countries grows.

In international trade, the same development takes place that we know from the different development of cities and the country side and the resulting rural exodus. Manufacturing and service providers are concentrated in the cities. The neglect of villages can only be prevented by significant infrastructure support and agricultural subsidies.

In the European framework the industrial countries also benefit more proportionally than the southern European countries producing more agricultural goods. That is why the *European Union* can fall apart if the industrial countries do not acknowledge their relative advantage and are not ready to share their financial advantages with the other European countries to a greater extent.

The trade, logistical, insurance and other service competences are also concentrated in industrial countries and because far more money is made in trade and in the service sector than with the actual production, unequal economic development is accelerated in the framework of international trade relations.

Today, in industrial countries we also experience ourselves the way the concentration of commercial retailers, logistical and other service providers in individual countries can disrupt the international equilibrium with companies such as Google, Facebook and Amazon. The resulting problems cannot be solved through the simple belief in trade which is as unimpeded as possible. In relation to the developing countries this issue should have been recognized far earlier.

Insofar as there is even an improvement of the conditions of production and industrialization in the developing countries, undertakings from the industrial countries must invest there with the consequence that they also become undertakings and investors in the developing countries themselves, but then again also share disproportionately in the generated income there.

Today a certain industrialization takes place insofar as labor-intensive production, due to the cheaper labor in the developing countries, is transferred there. Aside from the fact that even in manufacturing the greater share of the profits goes to western industrial countries which use the labor, this development was first in essence also the consequence of countries with their own attractive market forcing through customs barriers businesses from industrial countries to produce in the country itself.

The industrialization effect was even greater for the developing countries when they simultaneously demanded that domestic businesses had to be involved in the production operations in the developing countries so that business and technical know-how could be acquired by the businesses in the developing countries themselves and that they could also take a greater part of the profits and thus also invest themselves.

Without these restrictions on international trade – and that already proves that the naive claim that international trade is always beneficial for all partners only has limited validity – today's emerging countries could not have developed this quickly.

According to the principles of an international free market the international exchange of goods is also supposed to be promoted by customs duties which are as low as possible. We have seen that the emerging economies only gained access to the industrial developments insofar as they contravened exactly this principle, i.e. forced businesses from industrial countries to produce in their country and to allow the domestic economy to participate.

For the industrial countries the general lowering of customs duties led to the less qualified workforce having to compete more and more with the workforce in the developing countries even though they cannot live according to the living conditions set by the industrial countries themselves with such low wages which, in Germany, is then compensated for with top-up payments as part of Hartz IV (German unemployment benefit scheme). This way increasingly precarious working conditions develop and even unemployment.

The higher earners and those who earn additional income from other assets can always buy additional assets while the lower income groups do not have any returns on assets and cannot generate any investment from their wages either. The result is an increasing relative impoverishment of people on lower incomes and thus a starker division of society.

The great economic savings not least caused by the unequal asset and income distribution – and that also means correspondingly lower consumer demand – lets the savings, insofar as they are not yet being invested in property and are not fueling share price increases on the capital markets and/or are being burned, flow into rationalization investment. Thereby, however, also promoted by the digitalization of the production processes, the unemployment trends and the precarious labor relations will rise further.

Rationalization investments turn labor costs onto capital income. Insofar as the rationalization profits are not passed onto the consumers through lower prices due to competition, the rationalization investments thus at least aggravate the relative impoverishment of the lower earners. It is therefore understandable that all successful grown in the past 20 years have all almost exclusively benefitted businesses, investors and the better qualified.

The lower the income duties and non-tariff barriers are, the more rationalization possibilities are favored so that if economic growth is actually generated by increased international trade, the former almost exclusively benefits the capital owners, businesses and higher qualified while the lower income brackets are disadvantaged by it. That means: even economic growth through international trade is not necessarily synonymous with an increase in the improvement of general economic prosperity.

While the lower income earners in developing countries and emerging countries tend to benefit from the relocation of the processes and the additional industrialization of their countries, the social tensions intensify in the industrial countries due to the increasing unemployment and precarious employment conditions in the industrial countries and make them vulnerable to alternative economic strategies such as those Donald Trump pursues in the US.

Against the raging protest of the dominant neo-liberal economic theory and the rest of the industrial countries, the current US president Donald Trump wants to bring back labor-intensive manufacturing capacity to the US and force businesses from other countries to produce in the US itself with increased customs duties.

This is so to speak a corresponding plan to that of the developing countries. The developing countries have to ensure that know-how and capital are generated within the country, the industrial countries must prevent that less qualified workers do not find an adequately paid job in the country any more. Because there is no country in the world in which only highly qualified or unskilled workers live. Every economy must be sufficiently diverse so that the different sections of the population find work. Greater diversification also encourages mutual fertilization of the different industrial and service sectors.

With that policy the United States damages its international trade partners. But also the American economy will have to overcome difficulties in adjusting. However, the American market is so large that it can afford a self-sufficient economy with relatively minor foreign trade.

At the latest when the businesses have realized that the self-sufficiency aspirations will become the rule at the detriment of the free exchange of goods because the rest of the world will have to react to the American isolation, the businesses will provide means of production in all larger markets. The possibilities of digitization favor complex production systems, so-called *Fragmented Manufacturing* in one country anyway.

The economy is thus less and less reliant on mass production in specific places in the world and on delivery from there to businesses for further processing. It is thus not to be expected that, in the medium term, the economy will flourish less than before, especially as less qualified workers will be in greater demand and can push through higher wages.

Of course, those workers are also endangered by the investments in digitalization. However, this would also be the case without the protectionist measures. Undesirable economic developments can, by the way, be better fought with state measures if not as much consideration must be put to foreign trade. In the US there have always been periods of isolationism and it was always latently present. The US also tended to employ its political and economic powers, even to the extent of corporate espionage, to push through its own interests.

It cannot be doubted that later US Presidents will again open themselves up to the rest of the world again. Aid funds for disadvantaged countries and natural disasters could flow again and the troubled US participation in international organizations could be resumed. However, in terms of foreign and economic policy it will most likely remain "America first". America would also unlikely allow a renewed exodus of industrial companies. The policy of self-sufficiency will be continued.

Accordingly, other regions and Europe need to become more self-sufficient, primarily to no longer be susceptible to blackmail but also in order to protect themselves from the spillover of crises in other regions. Woe be to those countries who refuse to recognize this insight! Thus, the blow by Donald Trump against a completely liberalized world market can stimulate economic crises in the short term, but in the long term contribute to reducing the risk of world economic crises.

VI. The illusion that chronic external trade surpluses are a sign of healthy economic development and do not need to be eliminated, and Donald Trump's contribution to overcoming them

Countries such as Germany, China and Japan enjoy chronic and growing foreign trade surpluses. The value of exported goods in the years 2015 to 2017 reached record surpluses: >> more than 240 billion euros above the value of imported goods <<[22]

Current account surpluses are rightly seen as a sign that the goods of these countries are in demand internationally. But if 240 billion more goods are exported than imported, that means that Germany produces more than it consumes and invests to this extent. How is that possible?

If demand for goods and services in Germany were the same as for incomes and services, then additional demand of € 240 billion would mean that either
1. Prices in Germany increase until the ratio of imports and exports is balanced. - One speaks then of an "imported inflation". - or
2. The Euro exchange rate rises accordingly, which has the same effect.
Since neither is the case, remains only
3. that savings in the amount of the current account surplus flow out of Germany abroad, i.e. that the current account surplus is offset by an equally high capital export surplus.

This raises the question: why are the savings so high? Large parts of the population are considered relatively impoverished and the public sector cannot spend enough on: infrastructure, research and development, environment, education, security, social issues. The reason is the significant unequal wealth and income

---

[22] http://www.bpb.de/nachschlagen/zahlen-und-fakten/globalisierung/52842/aussenhandel

distribution. Those who earn a lot do not spend enough on domestic consumption and investment opportunities and make their money abroad.

For foreign countries, foreign trade surpluses of a country mean a corresponding debt, as far as the capital exporters do not acquire property abroad. But even then, in the event of economic difficulties in the capital importing country or the capital exporting country or in international crises, there is a risk of foreign property being sold off in the short term and capital market turbulence affecting other economic relations.

For chronic capital importing countries, such as the USA, from which disproportionately many manufacturing companies have emigrated, workers cannot be employed or are only employed to a precarious wage and large industrial wasteland has developed in the course of time.

Even within Europe, due to German export surpluses, the debt of other European countries to Germany is growing. In addition, the German export surplus pushes up the euro exchange rate, so that especially European countries dependent on agricultural exports can export less to non-European countries because of the high euro exchange rate and are seduced, because of the relatively cheaper foreign products, to import them and to damage their own production possibilities. Consequently, it is not surprising that, for years, Germany has been called to reduce export surpluses.

Of course, since the German State cannot simply prohibit exports or levy export duties, a balanced German current account is only possible if domestic demand in Germany is increased so much that imports rise and / or German goods become more expensive and thus cannot be exported to the current extent any more. The latter would also have the advantage of reducing the need for skilled workers to migrate to Germany and may contribute to the development of the other countries, thus leading to greater international diversification of industry.

To increase domestic demand, the savings rate in Germany would have to be lowered. This is only possible if the incomes of the lower income earners and the socially needy and public spending increase at the expense of those who save too much and do not spend their savings on investment Germany.

State measures therefore could take the form of:
1. higher minimum income,
2. government regulations governing employee participation in company earnings in a ratio to executives bonuses,
3. Greater participation of upper income groups in general health and pension insurance (progressive to a certain extent according to the level of income and the pensions to be paid are capped),
4. greater progression in income tax,
5. very progressive inheritance taxes, of course with sufficient basic allowances and special rules for medium-sized companies. Inheritances distort the market economy necessary for the same starting conditions and are a major reason for the increasingly divergent asset and income distribution.

What was presented here on the example of Germany also applies to other countries with chronic current account surpluses, especially to China and Japan. [23] In China, the national savings rate is about 40% of the gross domestic product. This means that 40% of the gross domestic product either has to be exported abroad or has to be additionally spent by the Chinese State and / or private debtors. The difficulty for China is that it is not only subject to international criticism because of its chronic current account surpluses, but that the domestic debt is also steadily rising.

China, too, could only counter this fatal development if the super-rich were taxed more heavily, especially since in China, as an emerging country, government spending on the development of infrastructure and the economy must be much higher than in Germany.

So far, countries with chronic current account surpluses have more or less successfully refused to comply with international criticism. However, the vigorous demands accompanied by threats of sanctions by Donald Trump, could force these countries to a more balanced current account.

Of course, the already implemented and threatened US tariffs and import restrictions force a restructuring of the international flow of goods and can lead to growth losses. Ultimately, however, they can help mitigate the risk of a total economic slump in export surplus countries as a result of international economic crises. It should not be forgotten that in Germany during the last financial and economic crisis employment fell sharply because of dwindling export opportunities and the collapse of the economy could only have been prevented by scrapping premiums, government short-time-working grants and other state interventions.

VII. The illusion that the economy can be reinvigorated by a lowering of corporate tax and the possible contribution of Donald Trump to overcome it

Among the most popular election promises is the proclamation to lower taxes. Through this striking design everyone expects that they will have more money at their disposal. In addition, according to the neo-liberal view of the economy, greater investment, economic growth and lower employment are supposed to be triggered.

It is usually not mentioned at the expense of which expenditures the tax cuts are to be financed or rather it is portrayed so to speak as self-evident that, through the expected growth of the economy, tax revenue will increase enough to finance the tax cuts unless the tax cuts also aim at incentivizing wealthy foreign persons and

---

[23] For Japan see:: Uwe Petersen: *Die wirtschaftliche Krankengeschichte Japans* in: *Unkonventionelle Betrachtungsweisen zur Wirtschaftskrise II. Krankheiten des Wirtschaftssystems und Möglichkeiten und Grenzen ihrer Heilung,* Peter Lang Verlag 2011, S. 122-129.

businesses to relocate their tax residence into the country, thus the expected tax revenue is the diminution in tax revenue in other countries.

The relocation of businesses and residence countries caused by tax cuts can on the one hand provide a country with significant additional income and, in that respect, also increase prosperity. However, it also lowers the world-wide tax revenue by the amount of the value of the tax cut and redistributes the tax revenue in the world to the benefit of the country lowering the taxes. In terms of the world economy there is no additional economic boost and the own prosperity is only paid for by the tax deficits of other countries.

Insofar as the other countries then defend themselves against this and a general race of tax cuts is launched, the world-wide tax revenue decreases with the corresponding consequences for essential state expenses. The negative effects on state spending caused by this in turn depress the general demand, the development of infrastructure, discontent and even strikes of wage earners and thus also the economy in general and thus also hinders enterprise itself.

Whether and to what extent tax cuts – aside from the indicated redistribution of tax burdens – economic growth and generating greater prosperity depends on whether those who have greater purchasing power due to the tax cuts also spend these on the market for consumption or investment purposes and to what extent tax cuts are not funded by lower state spending. Thus, it must be assumed that tax cuts trigger economic consumer spending for the middle class and lower income earners, insofar as the latter even pay taxes, and for workmen also investment and thus further economic prosperity.

The assumption which is generally considered as self-evident that tax cuts trigger investment is, however, relatively unlikely in our times. The capital markets offer sufficient capital for the interest rates, even when supported by central banks flooding the market with money, have dropped to 0 %. Therefore, tax cuts for the benefit of shareholders and businesses would at most promote spending for speculation and the demand only insofar as it may trigger, for example additional property speculation. These, if anything anyway relatively weak economic boosts must be contrasted with the shortfall in demand insofar as the tax cuts were financed by lower state spending.

Generally, it can be assumed that the tax cuts in favor of higher earners have more of a stagnating effect on the economy unless state spending is not reduced or are even increased and the tax cuts are compensated by a higher national debt. Examples for this are the tax cuts of the then US President Ronald Reagan, which came with a significant rise in state spending and national debt. Another example for it is the tax cut enacted by the current US President Donald Trump while increasing spending on infrastructure, defense and a wall with Mexico so far as those expenditures cannot be financed by additional tax revenue as a result of tax residence relocation to the US.

Thus, Donald Trump's economic measures may be adapted to his policy of

"America first" without consideration of the effects on the rest of the world economy. The international economic problems caused by them can, however, be additional incentives to correct any weaknesses and to decouple the national economy from the global economy in order to no longer be dependent on global economic problems. Thus, in the long term, the danger can be decreased that crises in certain economic areas spill over into other countries and lead to a world economic crisis.

VIII. The illusion that lower government spending promotes economic growth

In the course of the development government spending has generally speaking increased in all countries as can be seen from the following table.

>>Figures in percent

Note: The figures can contain minor discrepancies depending on the institution and method.

Country	2001	2002	2003	2004	2005	2006	2007	2008	2009	2010	2012	2014
Belgium			51,1	49,3	52,1	48,6	48,4	50,1	54,1		52,8	55,1
Denmark			55,3	55,1	52,6	51,5	50,8	51,9	58,3		58,2	56
Germany	47,6	48,1	48,5	47,1	46,8	45,4	43,7	43,7	47,6	46,6	44,9	44,3
Finland			50,0	50,3	50,0	48,9	47,2	49,3	55,8		54,4	58,3
France			53,4	53,2	53,3	52,7	52,3	52,8	56,0		56,2	57,5
Greece			49,2	49,8	43,8	44,9	46,2	49,1	53,2		51,0	49,9
Ireland			33,5	34,0	34,0	34,5	36,8	42,7	48,9		42,8	38,2
Italy			48,3	47,8	48,1	48,7	47,9	48,9	51,9		51,0	51,2
Japan					38,4	36,0	35,8	36,4				
Luxembourg			42,3	43,1	41,5	38,6	36,2	36,9	42,2		43,8	42,4
Netherlands			47,1	46,3	44,8	45,5	45,2	46,0	51,4		50,1	46,2
Austria			51,1	50,3	50,1	49,3	48,3	48,7	52,3		51,5	52,7
Portugal			45,8	46,7	45,8	44,5	43,7	43,5	48,1		46,7	51,7
Sweden			58,2	56,7	53,6	52,6	50,9	51,5	54,6		49,2	51,8
Switzerland	35,0	36,3	37,9	37,5	37,2	35,4	34,2	32,5	34,6	34,1	34,7	32,9[2]
Spain			38,2	38,8	38,4	38,4	39,2	41,3	45,8		42,7	44,5
United Kingdom			42,8	43,1	44,1	44,2	43,9	47,5	51,7		45,5	43,9
United States					36,6	36,5	37,4	38,6	41,6	40,0	37,3	
Peoples Republic of China					18,4	18,5	18,3	22,6	25,8	25,9	28,1	29,7

- Sources used:
- Statistisches Bundesamt (German Federal Statistical Office):[24][25][26]

---

[24] Total spending of the state as proportion of gross domestic product (Memento of 7 June 2007 in the online archive) (viewed 1 November 2006, online archive)

[25] Statistical Yearbook 2010 (PDF)

[26] USA: national quota 2003 to 2013

- Deutsches Bundesministerium der Finanzen (German Federal ministry of Finance):[27][28]
- Bundesamt für Statistik (German Federal Statistical Office) :[29]
- Technische Universität Chemnitz (Technical University Chemnitz):[30]
- Statista GmbH:[31] <<32

Along the reasoning of neoliberalists that low taxes invigorate the economy; the economy also flourishes more the lower the national quota is. Because in that case the consumers and businesses have a greater share in the gross domestic product, can therefore spend and invest more and thus invigorate the economy. Indeed, it is even argued that tax revenue also increases due to the greater growth so that government spending would not need to be reduced by the same amount the tax cuts are worth.

According to Wikipedia there is >>no consensus among representatives of economic science whether a low national quota also leads to higher economic growth. Thus, critics of a low national quota point to the Scandinavian countries which, in some cases, may have a national quota over 50% but also possess high living standards above the average. [33] So far there is no study which could prove a definitive correlation between national quota and growth. [34] <<35

>> Rising national quotas are depicted by Wagner's law. One explanation is provided by the Peacock-Wiseman hypothesis. Another explanation is given by Niskanen's budget maximization model.

Popitz' law postulates a correlation between rising national quotas and a rising share of the central state in the overall spending. Baumol's cost disease model also belongs in this context.

Yet another explanation attempt is the designation of government benefits as "superior goods". These are defined by the fact that their consumption increases with

---

27 tax ratio in international comparison German Bundesministerium der Finanzen (Federal Ministry of Finance) on the basis of "Statistical annex on the European economy" of the European Commission

28 Generation of the national quota. Bundesministerium der Finanzen (German Federal Ministry of Finance)

29 Figures in % of GDP. Statistics Kennzahlen in % des BIP. Statistik Schweiz (Statistics Switzerland), viewed on 3 November 2011

30 National quota in international comparison (Memento of 12 January 2014 in online archive) (PDF; 42 kB)

31 European Union: national quotas in the Member States in the year 2014, China: national quota between 2005 and 2015

32 Quoted according to https://de.wikipedia.org/wiki/Staatsquote

33 Germany on its way to socialism. in: .11 January 2010. https://www.onthisday.com/date/2010/january/11

34 How high should the national quota be? in: Die Zeit. 26 June 2007.

35 Cited based on https://de.wikipedia.org/wiki/Staatsquote

increasing income. If the demand rises faster than the income, the spending on these goods do not only increase in absolute terms but also relative to the total spending.

Further, the fiscal illusion is also discussed. It purports that citizens, without being able to foresee the consequences, vote for governments which effect high public spending. This is again mirrored in a tax system which is becoming progressively more complex which is supposed to conceal the actual financial burdens.

Brecht's law on the other hand finds a solution based on the constantly increasing urbanization. A further possible explanation which is not to be underestimated particularly in the western world, is offered by the demographic change. With a growingly aging population state payments are increasing which cover the attached consequences as for example the safeguards against old-age poverty, pension and health benefits. [36] <<[37]

These explanations may have some significance as to why the state has increased its spending. They do not, however, explain the actual significance the level of government spending has for economic demand. Because the more the possibilities for consumer spending decrease for the lower income groups due to the increasingly unequal distribution of wealth and in particular, as a consequence thereof, the income and thus the incentives for investment also fall away, the more important government spending becomes in order to prevent a gap in demand from arising between the economic supply and the economic demand.

The national quota also comprises the transfer payments to lower income groups which also mostly take direct effect as demand. Due to this necessity it is also clear why tax cut policies, as those by Ronald Reagan in the US and now again through Donald Trump in the US only lead to economic growth because they went in parallel with increased state spending financed by debt. Thus, a stimulation of private demand can only be expected from the lowering of the national quota if they come together with tax cuts for lower income groups. Nothing changes, however, regarding the overall economic demand because the government spending decreases by the same amount as the private spending increases. Insofar as the tax cuts are also used to make savings, there can even be a lack of demand.

Reducing government spending for tax cuts for higher income groups would cause depressions. Imagine that the government spending, including the transfer payments comprised in them, would be cut drastically in favor of tax cuts for the higher income groups; then the economic savings rate would increase further and the economy caught in a depression. Accordingly, a stimulation of the economy in a time when so much capital is on offer and so little is invested in real property that interest rates are moving close to 0 % is only to be expected from higher government spending financed by tax revenue from higher income groups.

---

[36] Berthold Wigger: The basics of economic science. Springer, Heidelberg 2006, ISBN 3-540-28169-X, p. 9–11

[37] Quoted according to https://de.wikipedia.org/wiki/Staatsquote

IX. The Illusion that public debt can be reimbursed and its consequences

Public debts are considered as a plague. A common argument therefore is that current generation should not burden future generations with their debts.

This argument is of course non-sense. Indeed, the future generation do not only inherent the debts but also the credit claims of the current generation. Similar to how debts and credit claims equal themselves in the current generation, they equally will in the following generations.

Anyway, why did public debt occur at all? Because the State sponsored part of its expenditure not through tax income but through loan subscriptions. Would the State have required higher taxes then mainly the rich will have been impacted by it, those who preferentially also subscribed to the share of the public debt. If the debts were really reimbursed during the next generation, then it will again be the rich who will be burdened by the reimbursement of the debt. Indeed, from poorer parts of the population debt reimbursement can hardly be required because of social-political reasons as well as of practical reasons.

The main fear related to too high public debt is over-indebtedness and the risk of sovereign default. This risk grows with increasing State indebtedness and has reached a considerable dimension, as demonstrated by the example of the following States. If we consider the extreme case of Japan, the debt has reached 236% of the Gross Domestic Product.

State	Public debt in percentage of the Gross Domestic Product		
	Year 2008	Year 2012	Year 2018
Germany	65	78	60
France	69	89	96
UK	50	86	86
Italy	102	123	131
Spain	39	84	97
Portugal	72	126	121
Greece	109	156	191
Netherlands	54	66	54
Belgium	93	104	101
Ireland	42	120	67
Danemark	33	46	36
Sweden	37	37	38
Finland	33	53	61
Poland	46	54	51
USA	74	102	108
Japan	183	237	236

[38]

The public debts worldwide encountered a special impetus during the economic

---

[38] IMF, World Economic Outlook Database, April 2018, 5. Report for Selected Countries and Subjects

and financial crisis from 2008 onwards. Gerhard Illing writes: >> For the time laps from 2008 to 2015 the IMF forecasted an increase of the debt ratio of the industrial States of a total of more or less 37,1 percentage points. Therefrom ˙he traces 21,5 percentage points back to the loss of revenue. Compared thereto the contribution of active fiscal-political stimulus measures (6,4 percentage points) and of the so far incurred costs for the support of the finical sector (1,9 percentage points) remain relatively reticent.

However, important disparities exist between the individual States. The costs of the rescue of the bank sector constitute in Ireland as well as in Iceland over 40 percentage points of the increase of the debt ratio. << [39] The German public debt increased by 236 billion €. >> This represents 8,1 percent of the current GDP. <<[40] But can debts be reimbursed at all, and if yes, how?

According to Say's law during the economic activity the level of demand, taking the form of revenue, pensions and taxes, will correspond to the amount of production of good and services. If the public authorities would not spend the tax revenue to reimburse the debt and would not in equivalent to their share of the national product acquire goods and services, then, in order to maintain the economic supply and demand, the creditors would have to use the obtained reimbursement for additional expenditures.

However, it should be considered as established that the creditors normally already cover their consumption. Therefore, the available means should be invested in real economic terms. Currently however there is enough capital on the market, as the interest rate level (price of capital) of nearly 0% or sometimes even of a negative value demonstrates. This means that we have currently a very high investment pressure. Therefore, the reimbursed public debt would probably not be spent, and the economic demand would decrease by the amount of the reimbursed loans which will have depressive consequences on the economy. As a consequence therefrom, the production of good and services would decrease, hence negatively impacting on the revenue and the expenditures.

Public debt can only be reimbursed when this remains economically without effects on expenditure, this means, it has to be ascertained that:

- the creditors will use the reimbursed debts for investment or consumption means and this, if possible, within the same economy in which the public expenditures for debt repayment are being reduced, or

---

[39] Gerhard Illing: *Staatsverschuldung und Finanzkrise – Wechselwirkungen und Krisenpotenziale* [Public debt and the financial crisis – Interactions and potential for crises] http://www.sfm.econ.uni-muenchen.de/forschung/staatsverschuldung.pdf, S.23

[40] https://deutsche-wirtschafts-nachrichten.de/2015/04/05/banken-rettung-kostet-deutsche-steuerzahler-236-milliarden-euro/. The German economic news claim that: >> The rescue of banks costs the German taxpayer 236 billion Euro.<< Actually in a first time it only refers to an increase of the public debt. If this public debt will impact on the taxpayer will be discussed and questioned in the further development.

- those who benefit from the repayment of the public loans should be subject to further taxes and charges.

The former is not to be expected because of the high economic volume of savings – not least because of the ever-growing disparities within the revenues and fortune – in comparison to profitable real economic investment possibilities or, because the investors prefer speculative market games.

For a higher imposition on the wealthy part of the population an increase of the heritage tax and/or a charge on fortune, which could be reimbursed over several years, could be envisaged.

Of course, undesired disadvantages or side effects may occur, which will have to be absorbed socially. In relation to inherited undertakings and family businesses special conditions should apply.[41]

Politicians are usually reluctant to use tax increases, partly because of the political power of the wealthy part of the population, but also out of fear, that this part of the population and undertakings will expatriate to fiscal paradises.

States like Germany which enjoy very high export surpluses are relocating the demand abroad and avoid thus the depressive consequences of a too weak demand within the country. Not only do they benefit from the surplus, but they can also to a certain amount reduce the public debt. But what does demand for public debt reduction means for a State like Greece? The economy *had* to collapse with the consequence that, as the table shows, the indebtedness of Greece increased even further.

In the private sector, overindebted undertakings only have a chance to further take part on the economic market if through settlement negotiations or bankruptcy they get rid of their debts or are able to reduce them by that much that a survival of the undertaking becomes feasible. of such undertakings usually recognize that it is better to renounce to part of the debt in order to secure the supplier or client or because bankruptcy will represent an even bigger harm. This reasoning also applies to States. The *IMF (International Monetary Fund)* rightly requested a debt relief for Greece and treated Germany as irresponsible for trying to prevent this step.

Now Greece is a specifically difficult case. Angelos Kotios, University of Piraeus, says: >>The high public debt of Greece has multiple causes. These are mainly the parallel economy, tax evasion, the complex tax legislation, the inefficiency of the taxation system, nepotism in the economy, high State funding to the pension system and a propensity to spend of the Greek political system.

Instead of effectively fighting this chronic and still existing pathology, the fiscal consolidation focused merely on tax increases and the reduction of spending. Thereby the global demand was decreased, and a recessive vicious circle started, which imposed further austerity measures.

Another cause of the Greek crisis lies with the lacking competition capacity of Greece; the reinforcement thereof was an essential objective of the adjustment programs. The means used were mainly the reduction of labor costs, reforms of the labor

---

[41] More in detail in my other publications, lately: *Blessings and Victims of Globalization,* a. O., S. 216ff.

market and the public service, the liberalization of certain professions and privatization. This reveals however, that this initiative did not favor the competition capacity nor the attractiveness for investment, because there are several way more profound causes for the unattractiveness of Greece such as the bureaucracy, corruption, over-regulation, legal uncertainty, closed markets for goods and services, State oligopolies, underdevelopment capital markets etc. Furthermore, there are also the structural causes such as the weak and limited production capacity, its orientation upon the demand within the internal market and the lack of a dynamic export structure, lacking innovation, an artificially blown and self-focused service sector (with an exception for tourism and sea transport), a weak undertaking structure etc. In this regard, the measures taken were not able to improve the profound and numerous causes of the deficient competition capacity of Greece. Consequently, the expected stimulation of the economy through an increase of exports – as a consequence of the decrease of revenues – and through the attraction of direct investors failed to materialize. While the adjustment programs were implemented the location conditions and the growth perspectives of the country decreased due to the new political and macro-economic instability, social tensions, lack of liquidities, pessimism, growing taxation and mass exodus of human capital. Generally, the adjustment policy of Greece focused too much on short-term objectives for the consolidation of the public finances and not enough on the structural and regulatory weaknesses and deficits of the real economy. All adjustment attempts so far were pro-cyclical and a converged national structure and growth strategy in the context of an integrated market-economic reform is still lacking.[42]

These economic deficits would not be eliminated by a simple debt relief. Insofar it was right, that Greece was forced to adapt reforms and structural improvements, which, already considering only the versatility of the causes, could only be painful. Simple aids would never have changed the system and the expended money would simply have disappeared.

Despite this, the economic policy cannot help but recognizing that public debt cannot simply be repaid and that in case of sovereign default debt reliefs are necessary. Therefore, from the outset debt relief should have been granted to Greece in case it realized the required reforms and structural improvements.

What is true for Greece is of course equally true for other European States close to sovereign default. The constantly increasing itinerant government bonds constitute a constant risk for sovereign default and therefore for economic and currency turbulences. If they cannot be reimbursed through higher taxation and charges of those who are also the creditors of the State, then every opportunity should be used in order to eliminate itinerant government bonds through debt reliefs

---

[42] Angelos Kotios: *Griechenland: Wahre Ursachen der Krise,* https://archiv.wirtschaft-dienst.eu/jahr/2017/6/griechenland-wahre-ursachen-der-krise/

Likewise, to the private sector, insolvencies, also through sovereign default and bank collapses should not be prevented. They allow States and banks to have a new start and reduce in a natural way the general indebtedness.

Naturally, social hardness and the destruction of vital undertakings should be absorbed.

Banks which are likely to become bankrupt should be nationalized at the value of insolvency and be temporary financed through loans from the European Central Bank or other rescue fonds until these loans can be repaid by benefits and the banks can be privatized again.

The losses from the bank insolvencies should primarily have been carried by the shareholders and capital owners like it is usually the case in a market economy. This would primarily have affected the wealthier part of the population. Bank deposits of private parties or undertakings could have, until a maximum amount which would have to be fixed, which would not put the saver and undertaker at risk, be guaranteed through special loans from the central bank, which would have been reimbursed through incoming benefits.

Obviously, the necessary debt reliefs would have triggered painful adjustments also in other European countries. As the other European banks, also those of the industrial States, got saturated in Greek and other Southern European government bonds, they would have had to accept consequent losses which would have let to the breakdown of some banks. Also, those banks would consequently have lost their defaulted obligations. They should also have been nationalized at the insolvency price and be supported and refinanced by the States and the European Central Bank and would only after their reconstruction have been privatized again.

How did the European States tried instead to solve the Euro-crisis?

Insofar as debt reliefs were permitted, it was taken care off, that primarily private parties of the concerned States will be concerned and not the other European States.

Otherwise, money was provided to States which risked the sovereign default, which served the limitation of due public debts. In this sense, they granted loans directly or indirectly through the *European payment bank* even of the amount of the due debt and thus overtook the risk of their failure. The high debts and the interests due on those hence remained with the States risking sovereign default.

Considering the amount of repayments which were due in the context of the so-called reconstruction, the economic recovery of the States was not only hindered but even increased. Indeed, insofar as they have to be repaid from the current incomes towards foreign creditors or creditors who will not spend the repayment in the country, the national demand gap, according to Say's law, will increase and consequently the supply will reduce. In this sense the depressive tendency further develops. Greece illustrates this evolution very well.

As the debt mountain remains, the risk of sovereign default remains as well, which dissuades undertakings and investors and provokes an exodus of the capital from these States.

As long as the Illusion that the public debt can be repaid subsists and that likewise to the private sector over-indebtedness will not be settled through debt reliefs or sovereign default, the economic recovery of the States should not be expected, are they remaining in a permanent stage of risk of sovereign default and impact the other European States. If the debts of the Southern European States would have been relieved, we would nowadays not have to fear economic turbulences due to a potential economic breakdown of Italy.

X. The illusion that money has to be guaranteed by gold or bonds and its consequences

The fight against the crisis and the development of the economy are also hindered by the illusion that money has to be guaranteed by gold or bonds. This illusion is a consequence of the history of the creation of money. Originally, merchants exchanged goods against goods. Accordingly, only a limited exchange of merchandise was feasible. Indeed, if a supplier of beef, for instance, wanted to get horses in exchange but the person interested in beef only had sheep the exchange could not take place.

Gold and silver served as general exchange resource, which also had a value for themselves. As these materials were difficult to be transported though different regions, and also because of the risk of theft, they were more and more replaced by bonds which could at any point be re-exchanged into gold or silver.

In the sense that exchange of goods grew faster than the exploitation of gold and silver, the payment with bonds grow significantly and allowed the possibility to use paper money in a constantly growing way.

Nevertheless, the illusion that the existing paper money should be covered by gold resources survived. The consequence of this was that, as long as the gold resources of the central banks did not increase, the amount of money and the related need in liquidities could not be increased, which as an end result limited the economy and restricted the economic development. For instance, during the 1920s >> France bought massive amounts of gold, in order to increase the amount of currency of the franc to increase the needs of the French economy. [43] <<[44]

But there was also the reverse development. Indeed, important amounts of gold and silver flow into countries after the exploitation thereof by Spain in Latin America or after so-called *war reparations*, notably after the German-French war in 1870/71; this led to economic overheating as the additional precious metal reserves caused an increase of the amount of currency superior to the demand of liquidities. The consequences were inflationary tendencies.

At the latest after the Second World War, once the European States had lost the majority of their gold reserves, it appeared that currencies still fulfilled their payment

---

[43] Barry Eichengreen: Golden Fetters: *The Gold Standard and the Great Depression, 1919–1939*, Oxford University Press, 1992, ISBN 0-19-510113-8, S. 4 ff.
[44] https://de.wikipedia.org/wiki/Goldstandard

functions even when they were not covered by gold reserves. Only for the American Dollar, which developed into the world currency, the coverage in gold was still upheld after the conclusion of the *Bretton Woods Agreement*. >>Continuous American budget deficits undermined at some point the trust in the Dollar. [45] This system ended in 1973. The 15 August 1971, the American President Richard Nixon revoked the reliance of the Dollar upon gold (Nixon shock). <<[46]

As the following evolution until nowadays showed, this revocation of the gold standard did not harm the US Dollar. Even though, the US and European States have again gold reserves, but those are stored in safes and have nearly no significance for the currency supply. Or did the European Central Bank oriented itself according to its gold reserves when increasing the money supply monthly by up to 80 billion €?

The attempt to avoid a depression and to stimulate investment through an enormous increase of the money supply also became the victim of further illusions: the believe that the increase of money supply automatically produces inflation.

In this sense, the creation of money was nearly compared with economic demand. Therefrom resulted the theory that the creation of money, as long as it is going beyond the economic payment necessities, automatically represents additional demand and therefore equates inflation. Still a few years ago this believe was presented by economic researchers as a scientific fact.

Thereby some factors remain underestimated:
1. The amount to which the additional money flows to poorer parts of the population which use it mainly for consumption means and which amounts flows to the wealthy part who favour savings;
2. The need in liquidities, especially of money market gamblers, which represents an important share of the economic need in liquidities;
3. The fact that also investment into currencies exists, especially, even more the more recogniszed a currency is. It was not conceived that liquidity did have a value on its own. This means that undertakings and private parties do not need to accumulate necessarily gold, it is sufficient if they hoard money in order to prevent inflationary economic evolutions.

Nevertheless, money is still treated as *bond of the central bank,* which does not need to be covered necessarily by gold anymore but at least by valuable securities.

Money, however, is not a bond but a *product* of the State which is used as means of payment. In ancient times beef and sheep served as currency, later on precious metals which were in a second time coined by the States.

Already with the coinage the value of the precious metal was linked to the *authority of the State.* This means that the coin did not only represent the value of the metal but also the authority of the State. With the issue of paper money, the represented metal value lost continuously its importance and, nowadays, it does not play

---

[45] Gerhard Rübel: *Grundlagen der monetären Außenwirtschaft*, Oldenbourg Wissenschaftsverlag, 2009, ISBN 978-3-486-59081-4, S. 157 ff.

[46] https://de.wikipedia.org/wiki/Goldstandard

no significant role anymore. A paper banknote is as much a product as an insurance policy, a construction authorization or a motor vehicle registration certificate.

On the one hand, the value of the currency is determined based on the importance and power of the State issuing the currency and, on the other hand, like all products relatively to its scarcity. The latter was already the case for metal currency.

However, as money and economic theories hold on to the fiction of an asset value of money, which means that money has to be covered by a material value, and that the product nature of money is not recognized, money is still treated as bond.

Central banks are dedicated to price stability and have in this regard an independent decision power. They, however, remain a component of the State. When they make central bank money available to commercial banks, they require therefore securities, preferably State bonds.

Insofar as central banks hold State bonds, they, themselves, finance the States. The interests on the public debt also gets back to them through the distribution of profits of the central banks to the States. In the amount of the State bonds hold by central banks debts and credits balance, so a net debtedness of the public authority does not actually exist. For the money given to the State is a product of the State-owned central bank. Nevertheless, the States bonds hold by central banks are still counted as public debt.

If the money made available by the State-owned central bank would be considered as a product, then the gross domestic product would increase and public debt would be reduced by this same amount.

Such an evaluation of money would equally benefit the overall economic account. Indeed, which consequence does the increase of the amount of money has on the economic demand and supply balance?

As already mentioned, all goods and services of one period have to be bought out of the supply provided resulting from the production of goods and services in order to guarantee an equilibrium. However, if income earners buy money or hoard it, even if it is only in order to increase their liquidity, this income parts lack from the general economic demand. If money was recognized as a product of States, then the income of the States increases by the net multiplication of money which can then instead of the payer of liquidity be spend.

In this sense, the current liabilities for issued money in the balances of central banks would be transformed into *sold goods* and hence, the national central banks would be able to reduce public debt in the amount of the creation of money.

The so-called *full money initiative* set itself the objective to provide recognition to the product character of money. In June 2018 a referendum on this issue was held in Switzerland with the aim of a transition towards *full money*, money which is recognized to have a product nature. Unfortunately, only 25% of the voters were in favor of this transition.

This initiative is also called *full money* because it additionally wants to prohibit commercial banks the possibility of book-money creation.

Until now banks only require as much banknotes as the level of risk that consented credits will be required in cash. As long as consented credits only circulate from bank to another through transfers no cash is necessary.

Therefore, the credits using only this transfer method which increase payment opportunities are called book-money. Most payments are book-money payments. All payments with a credit or debit card are book-money payments.

Cash deposits from bank clients and savings as well as their own capital can be borrowed multiple times by the banks. In times of crisis, however, it can occur that clients do precipitated withdraws of money which creates payment difficulties for the banks. In order to avoid this risk, central banks require that a part of the deposits, so-called *minimum reserves,* are hold by the central banks. There also exists regulations how many times credits in relation to the equity of the bank can be contracted.

The full money initiative[47] is bothered by the possibility of creation of book-money by banks and thus earning interest rates. It wants to achieve that only central banks can create money. This would mean that banks could only grant loans based on their currency deposits, own capital, private deposits and savings or money obtained through the central bank. They believe that the advantages therefrom would be:

1.   that in the context of the general economic liquidity need, including book-money, only central banks could make money available and could hence earn money through this which would benefit the States;

2.   that the risk of bank crises will be reduced as in the current stage of play a loss of banks mainly impacts book-money which puts the liquidity of an economy more at risk compared to the situation where banks can only borrow as much money as they themselves have.

A complete ban of book-money creation would expectedly seriously impact the flexibility of necessary money creation and of sufficient revenues for the banks. In order to reduce the risk of bank breakdowns it would be enough to increase the current very low minimum reserve rates (in Germany currently 1%) and the relative amount of own capital which has to be hold by banks compared to the credits granted (currently 8%).

An increase of the minimum reserve rate would also cause an increase of central bank money in circulation compared to book-money, which would provide additional means to States.

---

[47] https://www.vollgeld-initiative.ch/

B. The overcoming of political illusions and their consequences through a responsible European policy

Parallel to the rapid economic and social evolution of the last 100 years the potential for conflicts also increased. Traditional societies were pull of their social structures in the context of globalization of the European economy and society. The unequal economic development of industrial States and development States, but also agrarian States as well as an increasingly disparate income and fortune development in all countries discharge themselves in numerous social and religious tensions and provoke important migration waves in the entire world.
Undertakings operating worldwide and so-called global player won such an international power that national governments can hardly have any influence on them anymore. Emerging countries are increasingly pursuing international power and atomic power, which threatens the traditional powers. The damages to the environment related to the industrial development threatens to poison the World and cause worldwide climate change with unforeseeable consequences.

The establishment which is interconnected to the ruling economic and social doctrines defends itself from deprivation of power and preaches still the previous techniques for success, which turn out to be more and more of an illusion. Their doctrines and actions are perceived as lies by the so-called "rejected" of the society and provoke opposition and *alternative facts*.

What is true and what is false blurs, the rationality of argumentation disappears. A favorable floor for left-winged, right-winged and utopic Trumps emerges. Populist movements initiated by them become more and more popular. Through the election of Donald Trump as President of the United States, who is destroying the established order like a goblin, the chaos risks to escalate.

It would be another illusion to believe that the other powers will be able to maintain Trump and to bring him back to traditional behaviors. Indeed, Trump and all the other Trumps are the result of the breakdown of the former world order. The established parties and governing doctrines blame the breakdown of the Western economic and social system of values. They have to recognize that this system did not break down but that its form of the realization brought it to perversion. In order to overcome the economic and social crisis the objectives developed out of the European values have to be redefined.

I. Guiding principle for a European foreign policy

1. Strengthening of the European independent foreign policy especially through a decrease of dependency upon the US

From a foreign policy perspective, the unforeseeable policy of Donald Trump is especially dangerous for Europe because it can no longer rely upon the atomic protection of the US. It is also not excluded that Donald Trump and Vladimir Putin, disregarding the rest of the world and Europe, agree on an interest equilibrium at the disadvantage of all other States. Indeed, a relaxation of the tensions between the US and Russia could favor the world peace, but it is not sure at what price.

Opinions diverge about the usefulness of NATO as a defense union. It was created back then in order to face the threat of an extension of the East-bloc towards the West. Despite this the NATO was not dissolved after the end of the Cold War, the military spending was only significantly reduced. Following the Ukraine-conflict the perceived threat re-emerged, especially in Eastern European States, which led to the increase of military spending.

As demonstrated, the fear of an expansion of Russia is not founded. In case the fear is still perceived by parts of the population or individual States and therefore the US membership and its atomic umbrella become indispensable, then the defense efforts of the European States should equalize the American protection. Especially Germany has to increase its, compared to the GDP, relative slow defense budget.

Europe should not be militarily or politically depended upon blackmail attempts by the US. Therefore, the common defense should also be independent in organizational terms from the US and take the form of European troops, which allows the maintenance of independent armies but which allows the common actions – also within the NATO – under a single command. An intensification of the military cooperation between European States promotes also the European integration as such.

Europe should not develop any ambition to act as a world police like the US but favor everywhere the resolution of conflicts through diplomatic means. Nevertheless, terrorist groups, especially in Africa and the Middle East, could require military interventions if the local governments are not competent enough to face them and if the US are not available.

Not all the projects have to be supported by all States. In given situation, it might be reasonable that only one or a few European States intervene militarily, depending on the special link between it and the crisis region, and that the other States favor a diplomatic approach. In general, and some might regret this, the peace-making potential of Europe is more important the better Europe *could* intervene militarily.

Until which level the defense spending should be increased can be evaluated having regard the potential threats and other common duties. Favorably should be exploited the military potential of economy of scales and of common equipment.

Very urgent for Europe are also the peace-making in the Middle East and the termination of the conflict between Ukraine and Russia. The solution to both conflicts is not only limited through different interests but even more thought the insistence of principles. This concerns mainly the position of Russia, which is the key to the conflict in Syria and the Ukraine. Russia also wishes to find solutions to these conflicts.

2. Guiding principles for a European Middle East policy

Europe might have participated in the fight of the IS in the middle East conflict, but in relation to a peace-building solution it only has illusionary ideas of the democratization of Syria. Especially the Islamists other than IS which cooperate in the secular resistance against the Assad-regime, but which have hardly diverging objectives and therefore would also be against a democratization, are underestimated

The Russian policy was more realistic. Russia sees the only way of pacifying the middle East through a restoration of the relatively secular international recognized Syria. Syria is dominated by a religious minority: the Alawites. However, the Sunni religious majority is recognized and as much as other religious groups they are allowed to practice their believes, therefore they support Assad. The constantly re-emerging resistance groups, originating from the Sunni majority, are constantly and brutally suppressed.

Unfortunately, it has to be questioned whether an alternative regime to the force is possible regarding the fanaticism of Islamists, their atavistic State of God ideal and the, at least latent acceptance of the use or force? What would have become of Chechenia and Egypt if Vladimir Putin or al Sissi did not use the force against the Islamists, and not only for these two countries but for the entire world?

As already mentioned, when evaluating relations in these States it has to be borne in mind that in case of a change of power alternative forces may exercise the power, however, according to the experience the so far oppressed will themselves become oppressors, sometimes even worse than the precedent. Anyway, a restored Syria should rather evolve towards a democratic and secular State than a Syria dominated by Islamists.

Therefore, Europe should act towards a resignation of the Assad clan at the latest after the transition. In principle, however, a reformation of the former Syria would be the ideal solution which would also satisfy Israel and the US. The Kurds should keep their hardly obtained autonomous regions, especially as they follow a rather secular policy.

In relation to Iran Europe should keep its policy line, also in order not to lose its credibility; but it should not disregard the fact that Iran is reinforcing its missiles development and is winning political and religious influence over Iraq, Syria, Lebanon, the Hamas in Gaza and Yemen which could provoke potential conflicts with Israel and Saudi Arabia. Europe should therefore take a diplomatic advantage of the sever sanction policy of the US which aims at the favoring of Iran's negotiation willingness.

Turkey has a key position in the Middle East conflict. The dreams pursued by Ecip Erdogan to reconstruct the Ottoman Empire and its limited vision of Turkish nationalism is not only a restriction but also a threat to peace in the Middle East. Also, in this context, the sanction policy pursued by Donald Trump could contribute to the peace-building.

The aim should be that Erdogan makes again a step towards the Kurds and accept the once launched peace negotiations. The basis for such negotiations could be the propositions send by the since 2007 imprisoned Kurd leader Abdullah Ocalan to the international conference "EU, the Turkey and the Kurds":
>>
As a solution, Abdullah Ocalan makes the following suggestions: '
1. The Kurdish question should be treated as a fundamental question of democratization, the Kurdish identity should be guaranteed by law and constitution. A mere article in the new constitution with the wording "The Constitution of the Turkish Republic recognizes the existence and expression of all cultures in a democratic way" would already fulfill this demand.
2. Linguistic and cultural rights should be protected by law. There should be no restriction for radio, television and press. Kurdish and other language programs should be subject to the same rules and institutions as Turkish radio and television broadcasts. Also, for cultural activities, the same laws and procedures should apply.
3. Kurdish should be used as a school language in primary schools. Anyone who wants this should be able to train their child in such schools. In grammar schools, sub-units on Kurdish culture, language and literature should be offered as optional subjects. At universities, however, institutes for Kurdish language, literature, culture and history should be set up.
4. All obstacles to freedom of expression and organization should be removed and all conditions for free political activity should be created. Even with issues that touch on the Kurdish question, these freedoms must apply without restrictions.
5. The party and electoral laws should be democratized and guaranteed so that the Kurdish people and all democratic forces can participate in their own free will in the formation of democratic will.
6. By adopting a democratic local government law, democracy should be deepened and broadened.
7. The village protection system and the illegitimate gangs that have settled in the state must be dissolved.
8. The return of the inhabitants forced out of their villages under duress during the war should be allowed. For this, the necessary administrative, legal, economic and social measures must be taken. In addition, a campaign for economic development should be launched and the prosperity level of the Kurds should be raised through incentives and other measures.

9. A law for social peace and democratic participation should be adopted. It
was intended to allow guerrilla fighters, detainees and those who had to go
into exile to participate in a democratic, political life without preconditions.<<.<<[48]

I further develop the problematic of the Kurds in my book: *Blessing and victims
of globalization.*[49]

3. The Ukraine conflict

In relation to Crimea it has already been demonstrated why a restitution to Ukraine
is excluded. As both parties will hold their positions the only solution remains an
agreement to disagree with the will on both sides not to let this disagreement influence future relations.

The conflicts over the Donets Basin can only be resolved if the Ukraine agrees
not to become a member of the European Union and of NATO. At the same time,
Ukraine should be transformed into a federation, such as Germany, allowing every
region to have a cultural independence. Economically, the Ukraine could develop
into a bridge State between East and West.

The security within Ukraine could be granted through a guarantee of NATO and
Russia. In this case all sanctions against Russia could be withdrawn and the economic relations between Ukraine and Russia could fruitfully evolve.

The main opponent to the Ukrainian solution is Ukraine itself as well as the Baltic
States and Poland. The Baltic States are probably still traumatized by their annexa-
tion by Russia and the former Soviet Union.

Poland has always considered itself as Russia's competition and considers itself
as the real place of origin of the Slavic tradition. Russia was considered as violent
Asian power. Furthermore, the countries are distinguished by their religious influences. Polish people are mainly Roman Catholics and Russians mainly orthodox.
Consequently, they have the tendency to qualify each other as Christian heretics.

The Russia-phobia became nearly pathologic under the leader of the current governing party *PiS Law and Justice* Jarosław Aleksander Kaczyński and his cult for
his twin brother and former President Lech Kaczyński who died during the plane
crash in Smolensk and the accusation that Russia organized the crash.

If the Eastern European States should make their consent depending upon additional security guarantees, then they should be accepted and granted by Russia.

America's Russia-phobia is so strong that they could be interested in the maintenance of the Ukraine conflict as it offers the possibility to maintain sanctions against
Russia and to consequently weaken it in order to introduce itself as alternative energy

---

[48] Abdullah Öcalan: *Lösungsvorschläge für die kurdische Frage in der Türkei*, 2007,
http://freedom-for-ocalan.com/deutsch/download/vorschlaege-fuer-eine-politische-loesung.pdf.
[49] Uwe Petersen: *Blessings and Victims of Globalization*, S. 150-154.

provider. Donald Trump's accusations against Germany should be noticed in this regard that energy import makes Russia rich.

Considering such an interest, the US could associate with Russia's Eastern European neighbors and re-equip Ukraine militarily and split Europe as a consequence.

Donald Trump might be considering these options, but, contrary to the American establishment, he might be interested in negotiations with Russia in order to achieve a global solution also in regard of the Middle East and might be disposed to sacrifice Crimea.

The retreat of the US from the world policy was already perceivable before the election of Donald Trump and he only radicalized it. It forces Europe to focus more on Eurasia. Therefore, some illusions have to be overcome:

1. that in Russia and China the same social values than in Europe should be applied. This does not mean that liberal social principal should not be admonished from time to time. They should only in a limited way be politically influenced;

2. that Crimea should be reintegrated into Russia;

3. that Europe can still rely on the atomic and military protection of the US. Therefore, Europe has to become as soon as possible militarily independent. Of course, Europe favor the diplomatic crisis resolution. But the resolution possibility multiple when Europe also has an important military strength.

II. Guiding principles for a European refugee policy

For all true human beings, it is unbearable when people have to flee their countries and die of thirst, drown, are rubbed by gangsters or killed on their way towards secured territories. Therefore, it is a natural human obligation to help such people. Such a help can only extent to the point that the acceptance of refugees does not destabilize the host States.

You have to picture the rejection of a townsman who is moving to a village and does not manage to be integrated in the community. For instance, the feelings of Swabians towards Berlin inhabitants or of the population of Schleswig-Holsteiner towards Southern Germany illustrate this fact. Considering this, the integration of people from other countries, cultures and religions faces considerable difficulties.

Feeling of strangeness, which can evolve even towards aggression, are also experienced by the immigrant. When they are not coming on their own and are hence forced to integrate in order not to become lonely, foreigners create, according to experience, parallel societies: see for instance German-Russians before in Russia and nowadays in Germany, Chinatowns, Turks in Germany to quote only a few examples. Based on the example of Turks in Germany, who live there already for several generations, it can be observed how hard the integration of foreigners can be.

If the foreigners constitute manageable groups, then the societies can adapt to this, as the Germans constituted own communities and cohabited with the Russians. On the opposite, if they arrive in gigantic droves, then the helpfulness of the host

States is more and more undermined, and conflicts arise. In this sense, in Europe even the proverbial cosmopolitism of the Scandinavians reaches its limits.

In such a situation remains only a major isolation. This can only be loosened if and to the extent that:

1. the social assistance for less well-off are raised and that enough living room is created in order to avoid social envy towards refugees.
2. only such refugees who accept the conditions and behaviors of the host State, also towards women, and learn the German language get a permanent right of residence.
3. Initiatives for the integration of refugees are massively created and supported, especially in rural regions.

Only when the integration of refugees is achieved, they can constitute an enrichment and at the same time promote the relations with and the development of their home countries.

Furthermore, everything feasible should be done in order to improve the living conditions of the refugees in their home countries in order to eliminate the origin of the refugee flow.

In the curse of such a policy, the use of hardship should be refrained from. The refugee camps outside of Europe should be created as planned so that legitime asylum-seekers can be chosen and be safely transported to Europe. Still, the risk of refugees dying while fleeing to Europe despite all warnings and dangers cannot be eliminated. The help given to refugees has to be balanced with the potential destabilization of the home State.

As long as these realisations are not considered by do-gooders and cosmopolis enthusiasts, especially the German parties of the Greens and „Die Linke", a party like the AfD is necessary for the unsatisfied population to express themselves. Despite all resistance against the xenophobia in the AfD, it has to be noticed that if the AfD would not exist even more radical groups with violent tendencies would destabilize the society.

III. Guiding principles for a European economic and development policy

1. Guiding principles for a European external trade policy

The scientific, technical and economic evolution made Europe and North America leading States in the world. In the course of globalization, Western achievements were spread all over the world. Thereby the production places were delocalized in developing and emerging countries with the consequence that less qualified workers in the own State were in competition with less qualified workers from developing countries and hence became unemployed or relatively impoverished.

The differences in salary and fortunes were increased by the fact that citizens could save more money the more they were earning and hence hoarded a fortune which provided them with additional capital incomes and basic pensions.

All industrialized countries suffer from this division within the society. Beneath others, one consequence of delocalization of production towards low salary countries the US and the UK suffer from an excess of imports. The disappearance of attractive workplaces for less qualified, their social relegation and increase of their social need plus the foreign infiltration though refugee flows had as a consequence the formation of extreme left movements in industrial countries.

Donald Trump's claim to reintroduce high custom duties in order to protect traditional production and make them competitive again in order to reduce social tensions within the country is understandable. The demand contingent on the foreign trade barriers of less qualified workers increases the demand of workers and reinforces the trade unions, so that they are able to push through higher salaries and that the benefits from the production progress and rationalization do not longer only benefit to the capital owners, undertakings and higher qualified.

As a consequence of the aspiration towards self-sufficiency the international trade diminishes and the wage costs increase. Economic growth does not require more growth if the given market is big enough, even more so when there is a possibility of fractal combined production of all components at the same place. Therefore, it is to expect that the US will have an increase of the economic growth following the introduction of higher custom duties and the retrieve of the traditional production structures. All important companies will have an interest in a representation in the US and to be able to produce on the American market. Given the expected increase of salaries the buying power will also be more important.

Of course, the transition from the current liberal world economy towards self-sufficiency will in a first place cause some setbacks. In this sense the exports of American firms will naturally be reduced and they will have to establish production sites abroad because there the external trade barriers will also have been increased as a reaction towards the American self-sufficiency policy.

Undertakings and capital owners have to expect a very costly re-organization of their worldwide production network and an increase of salaries; hence they protest against self-sufficiency with the argument that free trade is increasing the general wealth. The illusion behind this theory was already demonstrated.

Due to the resistance of the economy and the still dominant illusion of the political advantages of a nearly completely free world market, the international political establishment sticks to this neoliberal illusion. The export surplus of Germany, China and Japan are criticized as harming the international trade; but without a Trump nothing would change. The state of the international trade is already also because of these disparities in the external trade extremely worrying and unstable. You just need to picture how during the next economic crisis the labor market in Germany will collapse because of these high German export excesses!

Even though the entire world hopes that Donald Trump will come back to "economic sanity", the probability therefrom is very small and even if in some instances he might concede, his policy remains an important factor of uncertainty for the rest of the countries on which no solid policy can be built.

Also, future US Presidents will only in a limited way come back the current liberal global economic policy. Indeed, the longer Donald Trump's economic policy is in place the more the advantages thereof with regard to the creation of new jobs in the industrial field, higher incomes and higher internal purchase power become evident.

It should not be forgotten that the US constitute by themselves an important internal market which means that enough mass production is possible within its own territory and through technical progress even complex productions become feasible at one location. Furthermore, American undertakings will locate manufactures abroad and consequently benefit from the economic development of these countries as they will have to establish there because of the high barriers on imports established by those countries.

If it is possible to rely upon the official announcements, then the industrial States are still in a phase of economic upswing. Thanks to Donald Trump the economic growth in the US even accelerated[50].Only States with no or unhealthy economic development, especially when those are reinforced by sanctions from Donald Trump such as Iran, Russia, or Turkey, are suffering from growth slumps, inflation and currency decline. Nevertheless, everyone knows that global economic development nowadays is like a dance on a volcano. The international dependency contributes to the fact that slumps also affect other countries.

Therefore, counter measures to Donald Trump's policy answering the motto 'what harms America most' can only disturb international relations even more. Furthermore, it would show a lack of solidarity towards others, especially countries targeted by US sanctions, if Europe negotiated special conditions with the US, notably also because the WTO-organization based on the most-favored-nation principle will be disturbed. It simply has to be acknowledged that the global economic relations evolve.

Demonstrations against a too intense international dependency exist already for a long time, and this for good reasons, and they managed notably to destroy the great Atlantic agreement TTIP. Donald Trump only reached the peak and forces a reassessment of the global economic relations.

No customs are imposed on products on which certain countries are specialized, such as the machinery industry in Germany, or the custom duties are paid without putting at risk the well-being of the undertakings. In this sense, the aspiration towards self-sufficiency does not signify the collapse of international trade.

Instead of regretting the disappearing trade exchange, Europe should use the possibility to create an even bigger self-sufficient market. Europe should also increase custom duties so that less qualified workers can find jobs in the industry and that

---

[50]https://de.statista.com/statistik/daten/studie/14558/umfrage/wachstum-des-ruttoinlandsprodukts-in-den-usa/

Southern and Eastern European Countries can evolve into alternative mass production places and that job order production becomes more interesting and that through this the European internal market gets stronger.

A self-sufficient policy also forces to adapt the production quantities by, for instance, limiting the steel production to the market demand and not, like nowadays, letting the markets be over flooded by steel products from China.

Especially Germany has difficulties to overcome the neoliberal ideal and the objective of further liberalization of the world market because it currently benefits a lot from it. Germany's strength lies in the production of high-quality industrial facilities and motor vehicles which are requested all around the world.

But considering the future perspective of the German car industry: The German industry managed to uphold the production of diesel vehicles thanks to fraud on gas emissions and should expect the collapse of the market soon. If the car industry does not manage to catch up its delay in the development of electric and hybrid cars its future existence might actually be at risk.

With regard to the Chinese technological race, it will become more and more difficult for the German industry to hold its preferential position. Furthermore, the concentration of communication technologies and the thereof resulting logistic and trade activities in the US make production undertakings more and more dependent upon internet-trade firms. Therefore, it would be advisable to follow China's example and to support own European internet trading platforms.

Also, in Europe for industry workers or less qualified service provider the exclusion of competition with workers in developing countries will increase the general income level, with the consequence that the European internal demand increases and the economic saving rate decreases. This reduces the necessity of export surplus in Germany as the missing demand was until then delocalized abroad.

The European market, such as the American one, is big enough in order to produce all necessary products within it.

2. Guiding principles for a European regional policy

Such as the different incomes affect the income disparities, because the wealthier part of the population can save more than the lower income groups, notably because of their capital incomes and the tendency of the industry to bundle in industry cities and to leave the rest of the land impoverished, so will also the different economies of the internal market evolve differently.

If they are united in a currency union, then the relatively differently strong developments also influence on the common exchange rate. In Europe's case this means that Germany's export surplus increases the rate of the Euro with the consequence that the weaker countries can hardly export their products and are also restrained within the internal market due to cheap imports from none-Member States.

Therefore, it is necessary to support in a targeted way the economy in retarded States, and as long as this is not achieved balancing payments from the stronger Member States should take place like it is the case within Germany.

Of course, the agreement by the wealthier States for such a diverse assistance program can only be expected, when the assisted Member States commit bindingly to respect the resolutions and when the voting rights within the Eurozone are proportionate to the inhabitants per country. Central institutions will have to be established in order to grant economical supporting measures to Member States and to regulate them.

If the Member States of the Eurozone could agree on such a reinforced cooperation, the interest of the Member States not yet part of the Eurozone to join could be triggered which would enhance the weight of the Euro in the world.

Furthermore, it should be granted that less qualified employees, especially within less developed countries, are protected from the competition with low-income countries so that they can receive a salary adapted to the Eurozone such as it is already the case in the field of agriculture.

3. Guiding principle for a European fiscal and financial policy

Because of the growing differences in the distribution of income and fortunes – generated already by the supplementary capital incomes of the wealthier part of the population – a gap in the economic demand is created because the economic volume of savings is higher than the demand for goods and services. In order to compensate this, the taxes and charges of the wealthier should be increased.

The easiest way to achieve this is that all incomes are charged for sickness and pension insurance – relatively to the contribution capacity – so that the sickness and pension insurances do not only rely upon the income dependents and the employer. Especially in the course of the on-going rationalization, notably through digitalization and the increased reliance upon robots in the production and service providence, more and more undertakings can exempt themselves from the payment of social contributions. Also, recipients of incomes from capital investment or rents are so far not eligible for contributions to social security.[51]

From a fiscal perspective, the economic process is the least impacted by the inheritance tax. Therefore, those should considerably be increased, including sufficient tax allowances especially for small and medium scale family undertakings. The payment of the inheritance tax should also be stretchable so that it can be paid from future profits.

If self-sufficient markets, such as the US, Europe, Russia, China and other economic unions force undertakings to produce in every region then consequently

---

[51] For further possibilities for higher solidarity financing of social tasks see: Uwe Petersen: *Blessings and victims of globalization. ...*, CreateSpace ISBN 13:978-1934992727, S. 222 ff.

disappears the ability for States to force other States through tax lowering to equally lower their taxes on undertakings and investors. In this case, a unified taxation could be adopted in Europe which will of course take weaker regions into consideration.

Higher income classes could be taxed more and the necessary public spendings on infrastructure, social policy, development cooperation, security and research and development could be increased.

In Germany this would foreseeably increase the demand for services from other European States, which would consequently reduce the export excesses.

4. Guiding principles for a European monetary policy

It has been demonstrated that the creation of additional money does not automatically amount to inflation because undertakings and private parties also invest into liquidities, especially in times of chaos or with speculative purposes. Therefore, the level of liquid assets increases in relation to with the increasing importance of capital market gambling. If you consider that nowadays only a small part of the worldwide payments is attributed to real economic purchases and sales and that all other payments are dedicated to the capital market, it becomes clear how the money level can increase without causing inflation, or more precisely that inflation only occurs on the capital market and the stock prices make the value of real estate and other goods increase. Indeed, new money is available for persons who can provide securities, which means already rich persons. On the real economic market inflation only occurs when purchase willing people – especially lower income classes – get additional money and invest it following an increase in the demand.

This new insight, in contradiction with traditional economic theory, allowed central banks to pump important quantities of money into the market with the objective to enhance investment and to reach an inflation rate of 2 % which allegedly is a symbol of a prosperous economy.

However, mainly capital market gambling was enhanced by this measure and the economic demand was only increased insofar as profits for consumption and investment resulted out of these practices. More important real economic impulses were achieved through the increase of the money quantity only when, like in the US, they were used for the financing of the public debt.

The continuously increasing public debt is rightly considered as a plague. It can lead to sovereign default and negatively affect the entire worldwide economy.

A better understanding of the nature of money could eliminate this risk. Indeed, if money was no longer considered as a debt of the central bank – and in the end of the State – but as a necessary product created by the State for the enabling of payments, then the GDP would be increased by the level of money creation and this amount would be available to the State for additional expenditures, as it is proposed by the full money initiative.

Central banks' balance issued money as obligations so far. If money was recognized as a product however, then they would credit the State at the level of the obligations created through the creation of the money. But the proceeds from the creation of money should only be used for debt reduction. It must not be a license for unrestricted public debt and money may only be created to the extent of the liquidity needs of the economy. This will also eliminate European bonds from the European Central Bank in their portfolio.

The overcoming of the illusion that money are bonds from central banks and not a product thereof (as subordinated institution of the State) for the enabling of payments would reduce the public debt and hence the risk of sovereign default.

C. Summary

The post-war order with the US as a leading power and social value provider is considered sacrosanct. Existing limits and influence zones must not be extended. Therefore, the incorporation of Crimea into Russia constitutes a taboo. However, this principle was ignored by the West when it was in its interest, such as in the case of the separation of Kosovo from Serbia and the expansion of the EU and NATO towards Eastern Europe, or earlier the overthrow of Mossadegh in Iran, Saddam Hussein in Iraq or Gaddafi in Libya.

The Western post-war order has largely failed, not least because of the resurgence of Russia and China's rise to world power. If world peace is not to be endangered, then the illusions that western democracy and social order can be implemented everywhere, and that Russia will hand back Crimea to Ukraine must be abandoned.

The economic backwardness of developing countries and the Islamic resistance to the Western secularization of society and the resulting conflicts have triggered huge flows of refugees that endanger social peace, even in industrialized countries.

The liberal market economy, to which we owe economic progress, has perverted into a casino capitalism, which is only kept from collapsing by a constant expansion of the money supply.

Economic growth in industrialized countries almost exclusively means additional income for capital owners, entrepreneurs and highly qualified people. The wealth and income distribution is shifting more and more in favor of a few. The "relegated" must be supported by additional social benefits. Although the ruling doctrines of neoliberalism are more and more of an illusion, the establishment adheres to them and propagates them as being unavoidable.

The economic and social tensions, exacerbated by the influx of refugees, have reached levels where the pronouncements of the established powers and parties are so beloved by the people that more and more citizens even expect a change from simply lying monarchs, who promise to create *alternative facts*. Accordingly, the President of the USA, formerly the leader of the western community of values became the leading "lying prince".

The global establishment is appalled and desperate to deter Donald Trump from his political destabilization efforts. Instead, it should also be recognized how Donald Trump destroys the economic and socio-political illusions, paving the way for new economic and social initiatives. The US is a huge market that is becoming increasingly self-sufficient thanks to Donald Trump. In response, other countries, including Europe, must join forces to become self-sufficient economic zones that are gradually less dependent on the turmoil of the world market and US blackmailing.

As the US withdraws from world politics, including Europe, the Atlantic community loses its importance and Europe is forced to orient itself more towards the East. Europe should participate in the China-initiated "Silk Road Resurrection" project, especially as this project promises economic revival for all Eurasian States.

A stronger disconnection from the world market also opens up the possibility of ending competition between countries for ever lower taxes for businesses and wealthy people. The resulting higher taxes and contributions for wealthy people can reduce the increasingly uneven wealth and income distribution and finance the necessary infrastructure, research and development, security, social and development costs, thereby stabilizing the economy and society.

Overcoming the illusion of money and recognizing the money as a government product to handle payments would also significantly reduce the indebtedness of States.

Author

Uwe Petersen born August 2.1932 in Rendsburg Germany, 1956 Diploma in Economics in Heidelberg, 1964 Doctor of Philosophy in Heidelberg (supervisor Hans-Georg Gadamer, co-supervisor Jürgen Habermas) with the thesis "The Relation of Theory and Practise in the Transcendental Phenomenology of Edmund Husserl". From 1965 in different economic groups and in the economic promotion and strategical management consultancy. Since 1998 he deals mainly with philosophy of action.

Previous Publications

Das Verhältnis von Theorie und Praxis in der Transzendentalen Phänomenologie Edmund Husserls, Dissertation Heidelberg 1964

Ost-West-Kooperation- Möglichkeiten und Grenzen, Rissener Studien, Eigenverlag HAUS RISSEN, Institut für Politik und Wirtschaft 1974

Arbeitslosigkeit unser Schicksal - Wirtschaftspolitik in der Stagflation Peter Lang Verlag, Frankfurt/M. 1985

Finanzmittelplanung in: "Unternehmensgründung, Handbuch des Gründungsmanagements", Verlag Franz Vahlen, München 1990

Finanzmittelplanung, in "Gründungsplanung und Gründungsfinanzierung", Beck-Wirtschaftsberater im dtv, 1991, 2. völlig überarb. Auflage 1995, Finanzbedarfs- und Finanzierungsplanung in 3. Aufl. 2000.

Das Böse in uns. Phänomenologie und Genealogie des Bösen novum Verlag Horitschon-Wien-München 2005.

The Evil in us Phenomenology an Genealogy of Evil, novum pro Verlag 2014.

Raum, Zeit, Fortschritt. Kategorien des Handelns und der Globalisierung novum Verlag, Horitschon-Wien-München 2006.

Das Verhältnis von Theorie und Praxis in der Transzendentalen Phänomenologie Edmund Husserls, Neudruck der Heidelberger Dissertation mit einem Nachtrag: *Husserl als Handlungsphilosoph*, Philosophische Reihe Hg. J. Heil, Turnshare Ltd. London 2007.

Kreativität und Willensfreiheit im Zwielicht sinnlicher Erfahrung und theoretische Leugnung, Königshausen& Neumann, Würzburg 2007.

Religionsphilosophie der Naturwissenschaften, Philosophische Reihe Hg. J. Heil, Turnshare Ltd. London 2007.

Sprache als wissenschaftlicher Gegenstand, philosophisches Phänomen und Tat, Königshausen& Neumann, Würzburg 2008.

Philosophie der Psychologie, Psychogenealogie und Psychotherapie. Ein Leitfaden für Philosophische Praxis, Verlag Dr. Kovač 2010.

Wirtschaftsethik und Wirtschaftspolitik. Zur Lösung der globalen Wirtschaftskrise. Von der liberalen zur sozialliberalen Wirtschaftsordnung, Verlag Dr. Kovač 2010.

Anthropologie und Handlungsphilosophie, Verlag Dr. Kovač 2011

Unkonventionelle Betrachtungsweisen zur Wirtschaftskrise.
Von Haien, Heuschrecken und anderem Getier, Peter Lang Verlag 2011.
Unkonventionelle Betrachtungsweisen zur Wirtschaftskrise II.
Krankheiten des Wirtschaftssystems und Möglichkeiten und Grenzen ihrer Heilung. Peter Lang Verlag 2011.
Unkonventionelle Betrachtungsweisen zur Wirtschaftskrise III.
Was ist zur Lösung der Krise zu tun? Peter Lang Verlag 2012.
Unconventional Consideration Manners of the Economic Crisis III.
What is to be done for the solution of the crisis? Peter Lang Verlag 2013
Im Anfang war die Tat I. Die Geburt des Willens in der Europäischen Philosophie
Im Anfang war die Tat II. Vom Willen zur Tat Verlag Dr. Kovač 2012.
Are we Doomed to Secular Stagnation? Limitations of Supply-Side Economic Policies.2014,
ISBN -13: 978-1503319103.
Säkulare Stagnation unser Schicksal? Grenzen der Angebotsorientierten Wirtschaftspolitik.
2. aktual. Aufl. 2016, ISBN 978-3-00-054939-7.
Blessings and Victims of Globalization Economic and social development, relative impoverishment, unemployment, economic crises, right-wing and left-wing radicalism, religious wars, refugee flows and the responsibility of Europe,2018
ISBN 9781983773297

9 781731 249166